Kant's
Foundations of Ethics

Translated by Leo Rauch

The World of the Mind, Volume I

Copyright ©1995 by

AGORA PUBLICATIONS, INC.
17 Dean Street
Millis, MA 02054, USA

4th Printing 2003

Cover: Ideas from Kant's work drawn by Donald Krueger

This translation is based on the German first edition of Immanuel Kant's "Beantwortung der Frage: Was ist Aufklärung?" published in <u>Kleine Schriften von Immanuel Kant</u>, Neuwied, J. T. Haupt, 1793, and on <u>Grundlegung zur Metaphysik der Sitten</u>, published by Johann Friedrich Hartknoch, Riga, 1785.

Numbers in brackets are the universal academic text pages in Kant's work.

To order an unabridged reading of this text on audio CD (ISBN #1-887250-16-6) call or fax 508-376-1073 and visit our website www.agorapublications.com.

Printed in the United States of America
ISBN 1-887250-03-4

TABLE OF CONTENTS

WHAT IS ENLIGHTENMENT?

Enlightenment is our release from self-imposed dependence. Dependence is the inability to use our own reasoning. Instead, we rely on others to do our thinking for us. It is *self-imposed* not because we lack understanding but because we lack decisiveness: *Sapere aude!*[1] Have the courage to think for yourself! This is the motto of the Enlightenment.

Why do so many people remain dependent? The answer is laziness and cowardice. Even after nature allows us to be free of external direction by others, we still look to authorities to speak for us. It is all too easy to remain dependent if I have a certain book that provides me with knowledge, a preacher who provides me with a conscience, a physician who prescribes my diet, and so on, just so long as I need not take the trouble to think for myself. I merely pay the required fee, and someone will go to the trouble for me.

Most people see the road to independence riddled with difficulties and dangers. Those who have so generously taken on responsibility for us will see to it that we submit like animals hitched to a wagon, afraid of the consequences of taking any steps on our own. But our struggles are not so dangerous when we realize that we need them in order to learn to walk by ourselves; otherwise we might never try.

It is therefore difficult for us, as individuals, to work our way out of a dependence that has become "second nature" to us. We might even be fond of our own foolishness, and thus be incapable of serving our own best interest, simply because no one has made us try. Principles and formulae—those mechanical tools of rational use, or rather misuse, of our natural gifts—are the shackles of eternal dependence. To cast them off for a leap over even the narrowest ditch is risky if we are not accustomed to it. This is why few people can free themselves from dependence by their own wits and pursue their own steady course.

But surely it is possible for people to enlighten themselves. If given sufficient freedom, the process of self-enlightenment is almost inevitable. Even among the mass-educators of the establishment, there will always be some who think independently. Having cast off the yoke of dependence from their own shoulders, they will spread the spirit of rational discourse regarding the value and vocation of individuals. However, it is truly remarkable how an enslaved people, aroused by others who likewise were unable to free themselves, will still try to force its enlightened educators into submission. The process of enlightenment may well be slow. Revolutions may bring about a rejection of individual despotism and of greedy and oppressive subjection, but they will never lead to a true change of mind. Rather, new prejudices as well as old ones will direct the thoughtless masses.

To reach enlightenment we need *freedom*, that is, the least harmful form of what we call freedom, namely the use of one's ability to reason openly about things. But on all sides we hear the voices of authorities telling us what to do. The drill sergeant tells us: "Don't argue, just follow orders!" The tax collector says: "Don't question, just pay up!" The pastor says: "Don't challenge, just believe!" One master tells us: "Reason as much as you want and about whatever you like—but obey!" On all sides we encounter limitations to our freedom. But which of these limitations are obstacles to enlightenment? And which of them are conducive to it?

I reply: It is the *public use* of reason that must always be free; it alone can bring about enlightenment among people. Its *private use*, on the other hand, can be narrowly limited without becoming an obstacle to the process of enlightenment. By public use of reason I am referring to its use by a *scholar* before a *readership*. By private use I mean its use by people who apply reason within a civic office or function entrusted to them.

To be sure, some affairs of public interest require a certain mechanism whereby some of its members merely remain passive in order to achieve an artificial unanimity required for government—or at least to avoid destructive interference. In this, of course, we are not permitted to reason; but, instead, we must obey. But to the extent that we consider ourselves members of the public interest and of human society at large—let us say a scholar who addresses the public through writing—we can employ our reasoning without harming the affairs of the machinery to which we passively belong.

Thus it would be senseless to reason about the purpose and usefulness of a military command, for it must be obeyed. But, as a scholar, I should not be prevented from commenting on the mistakes of a military action and from presenting it to the public for evaluation. Nor can I, as a citizen, legitimately refuse to pay taxes or impudently complain about them. But, as a scholar, I can publicly reflect on the inappropriateness or unfairness of such demands. Likewise, the clergy has the obligation to serve the church by preaching its doctrine. But individual members of the clergy, as scholars, have the full freedom and even the duty to share with the public carefully considered thoughts and criticisms regarding the affairs of the Church, its doctrine, and its practice of religion.

No criticism of this kind involves a breach of faith. To the extent that I hold an office and represent the affairs of the Church, I am not free to preach according to my own insights but must do so by the dictates and in the name of another. I will say: Our church teaches this and that; here are the proofs it provides. Thus I will give practical advice to my parishioners regarding the tenets to which I myself may not fully subscribe. I do this on the grounds that it is not impossible that some truth might still be concealed in them or that, at least, they do not contain anything that contradicts my innermost religious belief. Otherwise, I would have to relinquish my office; for I could not carry out its duties in good conscience.

Thus, when I, as an appointed preacher, address my congregation, I make *private use* of my reasoning because I always do so with regard to a domestic, even if large, assembly. This means that, as a minister, I am not free and should not be free because I am carrying out an order.

However, as a scholar who through writing speaks to the actual public and thus to the world, I have unlimited freedom, even as a person of the clergy, to make *public use* of my own power of reasoning and to speak for myself. It would surely be an absurdity beyond all absurdities if those spiritual authorities were themselves dependent in spiritual matters.

But should not a group of spiritual leaders, such as a church council, be entitled to commit itself by oath to a specific unchangeable doctrine so as to lead every member of its congregation and thereby also an entire people from now until eternity? I say it is impossible. Such a contract, intended to close off for human beings forever all further enlightenment, is null and void, even if it is condoned by the highest authority, by state parliaments, and by celebrated peace treaties. One era cannot, by unison and oath, put another era into the condition whereby it will become impossible to broaden its (very relevant) insights, remove misconceptions, and promote the progress of enlightenment. Such action would be a crime against humanity, whose original purpose is precisely such progress. Therefore, its descendants are fully entitled to cast out such decisions as unjustified and criminal.

The test for a legislative decision lies in the question whether the people themselves would want to impose such a law on themselves. This may well happen for a certain period of time in the expectation of a better solution and for the sake of a certain measure of order. Every citizen, particularly the clergy, would be free to make written public comments about the flaws of the current system while its established order continues for the time being.

Once people have publicly gained insight into the current state of affairs and have validated it through the voice of the majority, their proposal should be brought before the authority. It would then protect those communities which, according to their better insights, have mutually agreed on a different religious orientation without interfering with those who wish to stay with the given one. What clearly cannot be permitted —even temporarily— is to have the process of improvement destroyed by a uniform, persistent, and unquestionable religious canon, which renders the endeavors of humanity fruitless and, even worse, detrimental to posterity.

An individual may well procrastinate for some time acquiring the knowledge necessary for enlightenment; but to forgo its benefit for oneself or for posterity is an injury and insult to the sacred rights of humanity. Moreover, if a people is not allowed to decide the fate of everyone, then it is even less permissible that a monarch decide for an entire people. But it is precisely lawful respect for a head of state that unites the common will of a people. Careful attention should be paid that all genuine and intended improvement be carried out in harmony with civic order. Thus all subjects can be allowed to do for themselves what they consider necessary for the salvation of their soul. The latter cannot be the concern of the ruler; rather, the ruler's concern should be to prevent any interference of one member in another member's effort to gain self-determination and self-improvement. It would diminish even the image of our Majesty if his supervision of publications interfered with the efforts of his subjects to gain clearer insights—although it may well be done in the name of superior insight. He would expose himself to the accusation: *Caesar non est supra Grammaticos*. He would be even more guilty if he demeaned his great power by supporting the spiritual despotism of a particular group of tyrants to the detriment of the remaining subjects in his state.

So let us then ask: Do we currently live in an *enlightened era*? The answer is no. But we are living in an era of *enlightenment*. Much still needs to be done to assure that people are able or allowed to use their own reasoning in matters of religion. We have clear indications that they are now being given the opportunity freely to improve themselves and to achieve mutual enlightenment by gradually removing the obstacles of their self-imposed dependence. In this regard, this truly is the Age of Enlightenment, the century of Frederick the Great.

This, then, is the mark and the stature of an enlightened ruler: to regard it fitting to say that it is a *duty* not to prescribe religious matters for one's people but to grant everyone complete freedom. Rejecting even the haughty label of *tolerance*, such a ruler deserves to be praised by posterity for having been the first to abandon the bonds of dependence for humanity, at least on the part of government, and for having left it open for everyone to rely on autonomous reasoning in all matters of conscience. Under such a ruler, the honorable clergy can freely and openly present its judgments and insights in the form of scholarship, unharmed by their deviation from the doctrines of their office. This is also the case for every other person confined by civic duties. Such a spirit of freedom will spread farther, even to external areas where it must overcome the obstacles of a government struggling against its own misunderstandings. A shining example inspires a government; under the rule of freedom nothing more might be needed to provide peace and unity for the common good. People themselves will gradually work their way out of barbarism as long as they are not intentionally and artificially trapped in it.

The main point of enlightenment, then, is our release from self-imposed dependence. I have linked this process primarily to *matters of religion*, the most destructive and lowliest of all subjection, because most of our rulers have no interest in being guardians of their subjects in matters relating to the arts and sciences. On the other hand, the attitude of a head of state who supports religious freedom reaches beyond it, realizing that even with regard to *legislation* there is no danger in allowing one's subjects to make *public use* of their reasoning by presenting to the world their critical thoughts regarding improvements in its formulation. Thus we are proud to honor the monarch who has given us such a shining example.

But only a ruler who is enlightened and not frightened of shadows, as well as in possession of a well-trained and large army that insures peace, can say: *Reason as much as you wish, but obey*! One could not dare say this in a republic. This is a strange and unexpected course of human affairs and also a general paradox. An increased measure of civic freedom seems advantageous to the *spirit* of a people, and yet it presents insurmountable obstacles. A lesser degree of freedom, on the other hand, provides sufficient space for the full development of one's capacities. Under its hard shell, nature will tend its most precious seedling—the urge and call to *freedom of thought*. It, in turn, affects the mind of a people, allowing it gradually to learn the *freedom of action*. Ultimately, it will also reflect on the principles of its *government*, which will find it conducive to its own ends to treat individuals, who are more than machines, according to their proper dignity.

NOTES

[1] "Think boldly!" Motto of the Latin poet, Horace.

FUNDAMENTAL PRINCIPLES OF THE METAPHYSICS OF MORALS

PREFACE

[387] The ancient Greeks divided philosophy into three disciplines: physics, ethics, and logic. This division suits the nature of the subject perfectly. No improvement need be made on it—other than to add its principle of classification. In that way we can be sure the arrangement is complete and its subdivisions correct.

All rational knowledge is either *material* knowledge, relating to objects; or it is *formal* knowledge, relating only to the form of understanding and reason itself, and to the universal rules of thought in general, regardless of its objects. *Logic* is the formal side of philosophy. However, the material side, concerned with definite objects and the laws that govern them, is twofold, for these laws are either laws of *nature* or laws of *freedom*—the former coming under the heading of *physics*, also called natural science; the latter coming under the heading of *ethics*, also called moral doctrine.

Logic cannot contain an empirical element. The universal and necessary laws of thought do not rest on grounds derived from experience; for then it would not be logic, that is, a set of rules valid for all thinking and subject to rational demonstration.

On the other hand, both natural philosophy and moral philosophy can have empirical elements. Natural science must determine its laws in relation to objects of experience. Moral philosophy must frame its laws as extensions of human will insofar as it is affected by nature. The first area comprises laws according to which everything [388] does happen. The second area comprises laws according to which everything ought to happen, even if these moral laws involve conditions whereby what ought to happen often does not.

Philosophy can be called *empirical* to the extent that it is based on experience; it can be called *pure* to the degree that it draws its doctrines simply from *a priori* principles. Pure philosophy, if it is merely formal, is called *logic*; but if pure philosophy is confined to certain determinate objects of understanding, it is called *metaphysics*.

Thus there arises a twofold metaphysics—a *metaphysics of nature* and a *metaphysics of morals*. Physics has its empirical element, but also its rational element. The same goes for ethics. Its empirical element could be called *practical anthropology,* while the rational element could actually be called *morals.*

All trades, crafts and arts have profited from the division of labor. No one person engages in all tasks, but each worker concentrates on a certain stage of the work process. This is differentiated from the other stages by the particular type of treatment required. Thus the work is done to perfection and with the greatest ease. Wherever the work is not differentiated and divided in this way, and each worker is a jack-of-all-trades, production remains primitive.

But we may wonder whether the division-of-labor principle might not be applied to philosophy as well. Does pure philosophy, in all its parts, not call for specialists? Today, philosophers are accustomed to please people by serving up a vague mixture of the empirical and the rational. Those philosophers who are empirically minded call themselves independent thinkers, accusing rationally oriented philosophers of ruminating endlessly. Perhaps philosophy as a whole would be better off if philosophers would heed the warning not to mix their different tasks—and if each were to pursue the task best suited to a unique talent and avoid turning into a dilettante by mixing them.

Here I merely ask: Does the nature of any science not require us always to separate the empirical from the rational part? Further, should an empirical physics not be led by a pure metaphysics of nature? Should a practical anthropology not be led by a metaphysics of morals? And should both leading sciences not be painstakingly purified of everything empirical, contingent, and material? This is needed in order to show how much can be achieved by pure reason in each case, and to show from what sources it creates [389] its *a priori* doctrine—regardless of whether such a doctrine is the work of all moralists (whose number is legion) or only the work of the few who are especially drawn to it.

Since my current interest is moral philosophy, I shall condense the above questions into the following: Is it not of the utmost importance to construct a pure moral philosophy that would be totally cleansed of everything merely empirical which might belong to anthropology? That there must be such a purified philosophy is self-evident from the ordinary idea of duty and moral law. Everyone must admit that a law, if it is to count as moral (that is, as the basis of obligation) must imply absolute necessity. Thus the command "Thou shalt not lie" is binding not only for human beings but for all rational beings. And this holds for all other moral laws. Accordingly, the basis of obligation is not to be looked for in mere human nature or in the worldly circumstances in which we happen to find ourselves. Rather, that basis is to be sought *a priori* in concepts of pure reason. Every other precept, even a precept which may be regarded as universal in a certain sense, can be called a practical rule, but it can never be called a genuine moral law if it is based on principles of mere experience—that is, if the least part of it, perhaps only its motive, rests on nothing better than empirical grounds.

Thus moral laws, not only in their essence but together with their principles, are to be differentiated from any form of practical knowledge that contains an empirical element. All moral philosophy rests entirely on its pure part. Applying this principle to humankind, we see that moral philosophy borrows nothing from anthropology. On the contrary, it *gives* to humans, as rational beings, *a priori* laws. These laws require a capacity for judgment sharpened by experience—partly to enable us to determine in what cases such laws apply, partly to give them an entrance into human will and an effectiveness in practice. This is needed because human beings are burdened with so many different inclinations. And although we are able to recognize the idea of a pure practical reason, we cannot so easily make these laws effective in our *concrete* way of living.

Accordingly, a metaphysics of morals is absolutely necessary. We need it not only to satisfy speculative motives and to disclose the origin **[390]** of the principles residing *a priori* in our ability to reason, but also because our morals deteriorate without reason as a guiding thread and highest norm for their proper evaluation. For when we approach an action we wish to prove morally good, its mere *conformity* to moral law is not enough; rather, the action must be done also *for the sake of* the moral law. Otherwise the conformity is merely contingent and arbitrary; for even non-moral principles will sometimes produce actions that are simply consistent with the moral law, although they are mostly contrary to it.

The moral law, in the pure and genuine form in which it has its greatest implications for practical application, is to be sought only in a pure philosophy. As a metaphysics of morals, it must lead the way for all else, since without it there can be no moral philosophy at all. A philosophy that mixes pure principles with commonsense empirical ones does not deserve the name of philosophy (since philosophy distinguishes itself from ordinary common sense by presenting as a distinct science what common sense grasps only in a confused way). Even less does such a mixture deserve the title of moral philosophy, since it thereby threatens the purity of morals and goes against its own aim of establishing a pure foundation for moral philosophy.

Let no one imagine that the foundation of moral philosophy has already been provided by other foundational works—such as Christian Wolff's *Universal Practical Philosophy*, published in 1738—and that there is no longer a need to lay out a new version. Precisely because that work claimed to be a universal practical philosophy, it could not take account of a special sort of will—a will that would be determined entirely by *a priori* principles—a will that could be called pure will. Instead, Wolff's approach is concerned with will in general, along with all the actions and conditions that generally pertain to it.

Such a foundational work is different from what we may call a metaphysics of morals through which we come to know the objects of thought in a completely *a priori* way. We find the same in the field of general logic, concerned with the actions and rules of thinking in general, which differs from the transcendental philosophy concerned with the actions and rules of *pure* thinking

A metaphysics of morals must examine the idea and the principles of a hypothetical *pure* will. Thus a metaphysics of morals is not concerned with the merely contingent actions and conditions of human will, via information derived mostly from psychology. **[391]** In universal moral philosophy, there is also discussion (although there surely ought not to be) of moral laws and duties, but this does not refute my point. The authors of this science remain true to their concept. They make no distinction between (a) motives that are truly moral, as presented by reason alone, fully *a priori*; and (b) empirical motives, raised by the understanding to the level of general concepts, simply through a comparison of experiences. Instead, for these authors, motives are considered without regard for their sources. All motives are seen as qualitatively the same, differing only quantitatively. Accordingly, they formulate their concept of *obligation*, which is not at all moral but is required for a philosophy that does not make judgments about the *origin* of practical concepts, ignoring whether they are *a priori* or *a posteriori*.

This is why I intend, at some time in the future, to provide a metaphysics of morals. With this intention in view, I offer the present work. Surely there is no foundation for the metaphysics of morals other than a critical exposition of *pure practical reason*—just as there is no other foundation for theoretical metaphysics than the critical exposition of pure speculative reason.[1]

However, the need for a critique of practical reason is not as urgent as the need for a critique of pure speculative reason. This is because, in regard to the moral sphere, our human reason can easily be brought to a high level of correctness and thoroughness, even with the most ordinary intelligence, whereas in the theoretical sphere human reason in its pure use is riddled with contradictions. Accordingly, if we want a full critical exposition of pure practical reason, we must be able to demonstrate that practical and speculative reason share a common principle of thought. There is one and the same reasoning at work, differing only in its application. However, such a degree of completeness cannot yet be attained without involving considerations of a different kind. For this reason, the present work is not to be called a *Critique of Pure Practical Reason*, but the *Fundamental Principles of the Metaphysics of Morals*.

Since a metaphysics of morals can have popular appeal and suitability for ordinary intelligence (despite its frightening title), I find it useful to separate this preliminary "foundation" from that eventual metaphysics, in order now to avoid some of the subtleties that will inevitably appear later on. **[392]**

The present work, then, is nothing more than the process of searching for and establishing *the highest principle of morality*. This search constitutes an activity that is quite distinct in its aim. Thus it is distinct from all other forms of moral investigation. This important issue has hardly received the discussion it demands. Surely my assertions would shed much light on it and find considerable confirmation if that highest principle of morality were to be applied to the entire system of morals. Yet I must forego this advantage. The correctness of a principle is not proven by its apparent adequacy, nor by its ease of use. Rather, such features lead to a certain bias that stands in the way of any rigorous examination of the principle itself, entirely apart from its consequences.

The method I use in this work fits the purpose. It proceeds analytically from an ordinary knowledge of morals to a determination of its highest principle; and then it goes back synthetically from an examination of this principle and its sources to ordinary knowledge and its application. Accordingly, the work is divided as follows:

First Section: Going from Ordinary Reasoning about Morals to the Philosophical

Second Section: Going from Popular Moral Philosophy to the Metaphysics of Morals

Third Section: Going from the Metaphysics of Morals to a Critique of Pure Practical Reason.

NOTES

[1] Kant developed his exposition of practical reason in his *Critique of Practical Reason*, published in 1788, and his exposition of speculative reason in his *Critique of Pure Reason*, published in 1781.

FIRST SECTION

Going from Ordinary Reasoning about Morals to the Philosophical

[393] We cannot think of anything in the world or outside of it that could be purely good—something that is good in itself, without qualification—except a *good will.* Consider *mental abilities* such as intelligence, wit, judgment; consider *character traits* such as courage, determination, firmness of purpose. Undoubtedly these gifts of nature are good and desirable in many ways. But what if the will behind them is not good? Then these abilities and traits can become extremely evil and destructive. Think of the *gifts of nature* that constitute our *character;* think, further, of the *gifts of fortune* such as power, wealth, status, even health, and what is usually called happiness and satisfaction. If these gifts are taken to extremes, they can corrupt us—unless we counterbalance their influence on us with a good will. Consider how incongruous it is when someone without a shred of good will is nevertheless blessed with material prosperity. Such a person, whether happy or not, is not deserving of happiness if a good will is absent. This shows us how central to happiness is this concept of good will.

Some qualities are actually conducive to good will and make its work that much easier. Such qualities have no intrinsic [394] value in themselves, but they presuppose good will. Moderation in our affections and passions, self-control and sober reflection—these qualities are not only good in many ways; they even comprise some part of our *inner* worth. Yet they are still a long way from being good in themselves and are not valued without qualification, however much the ancient philosophers may have praised them. Without a basis in good will, these qualities can become extremely evil. The cold-bloodedness of criminals not only makes them more dangerous, but also more revolting in our eyes.

A good will is good not for what it achieves, nor for its effectiveness in reaching a predetermined goal. Rather, it is good only through its own willing. Thus it is to be regarded as good in and for itself, and as higher than anything it achieves by serving some or all of our inclinations. Imagine that nature were stingy in its gifts, and that it left us without the means or the ability to carry out our good intentions. Imagine that we could accomplish nothing, despite our utmost effort. We would still be left with our good will. Having achieved nothing, it would still shine like a jewel, as something having full value in itself. Its usefulness in terms of its results can neither contribute to, nor detract from, its intrinsic value. Rather, such utility would serve as a setting to facilitate ordinary human affairs or make a good will more attractive to those not yet sensitive to its value. It would not be recommended to experts in order to determine its value.

Speaking of nature's gifts, we know that we have been given the ability to reason. That is, nature has given us the power to reason as a way of ruling our will. Yet we just spoke of the will as something whose value resides in itself alone, whose value is absolute and independent of its effects. Our will seems complete in itself and needs nothing further to complete it. But if this is so, then surely we must find it strange that nature has intended reason to be the governing principle of our will—for then our will is not independent or complete. Perhaps we have misunderstood the significance **[395]** of this arrangement. How shall we make sense of this?

In all living things there is a basic principle of purpose. Every organ is best fitted for the purpose it is meant to serve. Consider the case of a being that has reason and will. Suppose that it was nature's purpose, in combining these, to insure the creature's survival, its *well-being*, even its *happiness*. If this was nature's purpose, then reason would not be the device best fitted for that end. Instead, it would seem that all actions and behavior intended to serve nature's purpose would have been far better served by instinct, not by reason as a guide.

Such a creature, moved by instinct alone, could have used whatever reasoning power it had simply for the admiration of its own self and its Creator. Certainly, it could have done far better than either subjecting its will to something as weak and deceptive as reason, or using reason for nothing better than to interfere with nature's purposes. Above all, by relying on instinct rather than reason as a guide for will, nature would have prevented reason from intruding into *practice*, not permitting reason's feeble insight to lay out a plan of life's purposes and to decide (somehow) on the means to attain them. Instead of reason, nature itself would choose life's purposes and the means to attain them. Such is the case with most creatures, where all this is entrusted to instinct.

Indeed, the more our cultivated reason concerns itself with the aim of enjoying life and achieving happiness, the more elusive those aims become, and the farther we veer away from true contentment. As a result, in many people a certain degree of *misology*, a hatred of reason, arises, especially in those who are most experienced in the use of reason, if they are honest enough to admit it. When they add up all the advantages involved in using the mind, not only from the invention of gadgets that provide ordinary luxuries but even from the sciences (which ultimately seem to be a luxury of the mind), they will see that, rather than the happiness they anticipated, they have only brought more worry upon themselves. **[396]**

On this score we might even come to envy those people who are closer to their instincts, and who allow reason the least possible influence on their actions. In any case, reason is not for the purpose of insuring our happiness. Instead, reason can serve the far greater purpose of orienting our private aims to the higher goals of human existence.

Reason, then, is not effective enough to lead the will to all its goals, or to satisfy all our needs. Indeed, it even proliferates our needs; and for the purpose of satisfying them, a natural instinct would have served us with much greater assurance. Yet despite all this, we have been endowed with reason as a governing capacity that influences the *will*. The true function of reason, then, is not to produce a will that is to serve as a *means* to some other *end*. Rather, its function is to produce a *will that is good in itself*. Given that nature generally works for a purpose, we can now see why it is absolutely necessary for us to have reason.

Our will need not be the only good thing, nor even the entire good. Yet it must be the highest good, as well as the precondition for the pursuit of happiness. Accordingly (and we may see that this is consistent with nature's own wisdom), the cultivation of reason, as a requirement of the highest good, may even put a limit to our happiness, at least in this life. This is so because the highest good (that is, a good will) is unconditioned, while happiness has certain conditions that must be met. And even if the pursuit of reason were to reduce our happiness to nothing, this would not be against nature's purpose. Reason recognizes its highest practical function in providing the basis for a good will. In achieving this purpose, reason has its own characteristic satisfaction, namely, that of fulfilling a purpose set only by itself (even if this involves thwarting our inclinations).

We must now develop this concept of a **[397]** good will valuable for itself alone and good without any further purpose attached to it. This concept is already present in healthy common sense, so there is no need to teach it but only to clarify it. It stands in the highest place, as the precondition for all else, when we come to evaluate the entire worth of our actions. Let us therefore take up the concept of *duty*—which includes the concept of a good will, although with certain subjective limits and drawbacks.

Rather than obscuring good will, however, these limits and drawbacks serve only to emphasize it by contrast and so make it shine all the more clearly.

First, I set aside consideration of all actions that are already recognized as being contrary to duty, regardless of whether they may be serviceable to some purpose. There can be no question as to whether such actions are done *from duty*, since they are opposed to duty. I also set aside those actions that we carry out in accordance with duty for which we have no immediate *inclination*, but because we are driven to them by some other inclination. Here it is easy to decide whether an action that is consistent with duty is done *for duty's sake* or for some self-serving purpose. It is much harder to make this distinction where an action is in accordance with duty and we also have an *immediate* inclination to do it.

For example, it is certainly consistent with duty for a shopkeeper not to take advantage of an inexperienced customer by overcharging. A wise shopkeeper will avoid doing so even when there is a great deal of business and will keep to a firm price for everyone, a child or anyone else. Everyone is then served *honestly*. But did the shopkeeper act from duty, that is, from principles of honesty, or merely in order to serve personal advantage? Let us assume that the shopkeeper had no immediate inclination to be impartial or altruistic to customers concerning price, and thus acted neither from duty nor from an inclination to act honestly, but for the sake of self-interest.

For a different example, saving your own life is a moral duty. In addition, everyone has an immediate inclination to do so. But that is precisely why there is no inner value to our human concern on this score, and why the guiding principle of such an action has no moral content. That is, saving your life is *consistent* with duty, **[398]** but it is not something done *for duty's sake*. On the other hand, when adversity and hopeless suffering have drained all taste out of life; when an unfortunate person, rather than meekly accepting fate, no longer has any love of life and longs to end it — but nevertheless stays alive, not from fear or inclination but from a sense of duty — then the guiding principle has moral weight.

A further example: It is your duty to do good to others where you can. But there are those sympathetically inclined souls who do so from no other motive than vanity or self-interest. They derive an inner satisfaction in spreading joy to others and take delight in contributing to their satisfaction. I argue that such a case has no genuine moral worth to it — though the action might well be praiseworthy and even consistent with duty. Instead, the action is equivalent to other inclinations, such as an inclination to receive honor.

When our action happens to hit on something that is of general benefit and is also praiseworthy for being consistent with duty, it deserves praise and encouragement, but does not deserve moral esteem, since its underlying principle (its "maxim") lacks moral content: namely, the obligation to do such a thing not out of mere inclination but from *duty*.

Let us assume that the fellow feelings of our humanitarian are overshadowed by personal miseries, enough to shut off all sympathy regarding the fate of others, and that this person still has sufficient resources to help others in need, but lacks such inclination. Now let us assume that person forcibly overcomes indifference and helps others, not from any inclination but simply from a sense of duty. Then, and only then, does the action take on true moral value.

Let us assume, further, that nature has put all too little sympathy in the heart of a man (who is otherwise a quite decent human being); let us say he has a cold temperament and is indifferent to the suffering of others. Perhaps because he is so stoical in being able to bear his own suffering, he expects a comparable stoicism on the part of others. Let us say nature has not made him a natural humanitarian (even though he would not be the worst of nature's products in the light of his other qualities). Despite all this we may ask: Could he not still find within himself a source of value far higher than anything that a warm-hearted temperament could provide him? Certainly! Character is shown — [399] in its highest and incomparable aspect — in the fact that he does good, not from his good nature or inclination, but from duty.

It is a duty to promote our own happiness (at least indirectly). Dissatisfaction with our own condition, amid many cares and unmet needs, could easily provide a great *temptation to violate our duty*. But duty apart, we all have the strongest inner inclination towards the pursuit of happiness, for it is precisely in this idea of happiness that all our inclinations merge into one. Yet the inclination to pursue happiness can seriously destroy some of our other inclinations. This is why we cannot have a clear idea of what this total satisfaction of our inclinations (as equivalent to happiness) would be.

No wonder, then, a single definite inclination can take the place of an indefinite idea, especially if the inclination promises a definite fulfillment at a definite time. Thus, someone with a troublesome medical condition still might choose to indulge in what is detrimental and be willing to take the consequences, gaining the definite pleasure of the moment in exchange for the dubious possibility of restoring health (and happiness) through abstention. But even if, in such a case, the general inclination towards happiness has not corrupted our will, and the goal of good health has not shaped our thinking, there still remains (as in all the other cases) a law—the law that we must promote our happiness, not as a matter of inclination but as a duty. In this, above all, our conduct takes on moral value.

It is in this sense, surely, that we ought to understand the Biblical passages in which we are commanded to love our neighbor, even our enemy. Love, as inclination, cannot be commanded. Doing good to others out of duty alone, when there is no inclination to do so, and when there is even a natural and ungovernable disinclination to do so, can be commanded. This is love in *practice*, not love based on *emotion*. It is a love that rests in the will, not in the sway of feeling; a love that rests in the principles of action, not in a melting sympathy. It is this love in practice, alone, that can be commanded.

The second proposition is this: In an action done from duty, the moral value is *not in the purpose* of the action but in the guiding principle—or maxim—by which it is chosen. Thus its moral [**400**] value does not depend on its goal, but only on the *principle of the will* that governs the action—regardless of whatever outcome is desired.

Therefore it is neither our purposes nor their outcome (as ends and motives of the will) that can give our actions their unconditioned moral value. But where, then, is this value to be found, since it is not to be looked for in the expected effect of the will? We find it only in the *principle of our own willing*, irrespective of the outcome to be achieved by our action.

Consequently, the will stands at a crossroads, between its *a priori* principle (which is its formal aspect) and its *a posteriori* incentive (its material aspect). Since every material element of effect or outcome must be disregarded in any action done from duty, and since the will must be determined one way or another, it follows that the will must be determined, in general, by the formal principle.

Drawing a conclusion, then, from our first two propositions, the third proposition is this: *Duty is the need to act out of respect for law.*

Regarding the outcome of my action, I can have an inclination toward it, but I can never have respect for it. This is because I am looking merely at the effect of my will, not at the activity of my will. For the same reason, I cannot have respect for a mere inclination—whether it be my own or that of someone else. At most I can approve of an inclination if it is my own, even love another person's inclination for being beneficial to me.

But what I can regard with respect, as a command incumbent upon me, is something connected to my will as its source, but never as its effect. I can respect something that does not simply serve my inclination, but outweighs or excludes such inclination when I make my choice, leaving nothing but the law.

Accordingly, an action done from duty must leave aside all influence of inclination and every goal of the will. Thus there is nothing left that could determine my will, except (objectively) the *law*, and (subjectively) *pure respect* for this law as it governs practice. I call this the *practical* law. Therefore, there is the maxim commanding me to obey this law, even to the detriment of all my inclinations.[1] **[401]**

Thus the moral value of an action is not in the expected effect of the action, nor in any principle of action whose motive is drawn from the expected effect. All these effects (for example, the pleasantness of our condition, even the promotion of happiness in others) could have been brought about by other means. They may not necessarily arise from the will of a rational being. Such will is the only source of the highest and unconditioned good; and the highest good, which we call moral, *is already present in the rational being* who acts accordingly. Therefore, this highest good is nothing but *the idea of law in itself*, to the extent that it is the idea of law (and not any expected result) that determines the source of the will.[2]

What sort of law can this be? Its effect on the will must be **[402]** such that the will can be called good, absolutely and without qualification. Yet such a law must ignore all the expected effects that would result from it. Since we have deprived the will of every incentive that could follow as the effect of conforming to a particular law, nothing is left but the conformity of an action to universal lawfulness. This conformity must serve the will as its principle. That is, I ought never to act except in such a way *that I can also will that the maxim of my action should become a universal law.* Here the pure conformity of an action to universal law (without relying on any law prescribing a particular action) is to serve the will as its guiding principle. If this is so, then the concept of duty must retain its meaning and must not become an empty delusion. Ordinary common sense agrees totally with this when faced with practical judgment; and it always keeps the universal principle in sight.

Here is a problem to be considered as an example: Assume that I am in some sort of difficulty. In order to get out of the difficulty I make a promise to someone, but I have no intention of keeping that promise. May I make a false promise? This question can have two meanings: Is it smart to make a false promise? Is it consistent with duty to make a false promise? In regard to the first, which happens frequently enough, I can see that false promising is not the most clever way of getting out of my difficulty. Rather, I must consider whether there may not follow, from this lie, some inconvenience even greater than the difficulty I now manage to avoid. For despite all my supposed *cleverness* I cannot easily foresee all the consequences of my action. And so, if the question is whether it is smart to make a false promise, it may well turn out that the *smarter* move is to act according to a universal maxim that can become a habitual action for me: namely, not to promise anything unless it is with the aim of holding to it.

But here it occurs to me that such a maxim may be based on nothing more than my concern over the bad consequences. To be truthful from a sense of duty is altogether different from being truthful out of worry for the detrimental consequences of doing otherwise. In the first case, the concept of the action contains a law that applies to me; in the second case I must, above all, be alert to every possible outcome that might be connected to what I am about to do. If I deviate from the principle of duty, this is surely bad enough; but if I depart from the prudential maxim **[403]** of doing whatever is the smart thing to do, it might sometimes be advantageous, but it is surely safer to stick to duty.

Can making a false promise be consistent with duty? To answer this question in the shortest and least deceptive way, I ask myself: Would I be satisfied that my maxim, my governing principle (to get out of a difficulty by making a false promise), should become a universal law, applicable both to myself and to others? And could I really tell myself that everyone may make a false promise in order to get out of a difficulty that could not be avoided in any other way?

Immediately I see that I can will the lie, but that I cannot will that lying should become a universal law. By such a law there could be no promising, because it would be pointless for me to make a promise asserting my own will about my future actions. No one could believe such an assertion on my part, and if they did, they might pay me back in similar coin. As a result, my maxim would negate itself as soon as it were asserted as a universal law.

It takes no great ingenuity for me to figure out what I have to do so that my will is morally good. Inexperienced though I might be in the ways of the world, and unable to foresee all possible events, I need only ask myself: Can I also will that my maxim should become a universal law? If I cannot will this, my maxim must be rejected—not because of some disadvantage to myself or others, but because, as a principle, it cannot fit into a possible scheme of universal laws. Reason compels my respect for such a possible scheme—and even if I do not as yet *understand* the basis for it, it is open to philosophical examination. This much I do understand: What operates here is respect. This involves an evaluative judgment, which far outweighs all value stemming from mere inclination. Further, duty is the necessity for my actions to be done out of *pure* respect for the law that governs action. Every other motive must give way to this concept of duty, because it is the precondition of a will that is good *in itself*, and whose value is above everything else.

We have now reached the basic principle of moral knowledge, as grasped by human reason. Granted, reason does not set up this principle in an abstract universal form; yet it always sees it as a standard of judgment. Here **[404]** it would be easy to show how human reason, having this compass in hand, is able to distinguish quite well what is good, what is evil, what is consistent with duty, what is counter to duty—and to do this in regard to all cases that may come up. Thus our human reason does not need to be taught anything new in this matter, but only needs to be made aware of its own principle (as Socrates did). Therefore we need no science or philosophy in order to know what we have to do in order to be honest and good, even wise and virtuous. Each of us knows what we must know and what we must do. This knowledge is the common property of everyone.

Once we distinguish between our capacity for practical and theoretical judgment, we cannot help but admire the predominance of the practical over the theoretical in human understanding. In the theoretical sphere, if common reasoning departs from the laws of experience and sense perception, it falls into what is inconceivable and self-contradictory—into a jumble of what is uncertain, obscure, and unreal. In the practical sphere, on the other hand, the power of judgment begins to show itself as superior whenever common reasoning excludes all sensory motives from its practical laws.

Then the common reasoning becomes devious—perhaps even resorting to all sorts of trickery in order to square our conscience with what is to be called right. Thus it rationalizes our actions. In this, however, we have as good a hope as any philosopher of finding the right path. Perhaps it is an even stronger hope than a philosopher might have, because the philosopher can have no basic principle other than that held by common reasoning. Philosophical judgment can easily get bogged down in a mess of irrelevant considerations that may lead us astray.

Would it not be more advisable, in matters of morals, to be guided by the judgment of common reasoning? Should we not, at most, only introduce philosophy to set up a system of morals that is even more complete, more intelligible, and more readily applicable (especially for philosophical discussion)? This would be the opposite of the philosopher's usual aim of leading human understanding away from its happy simplicity onto a new path of inquiry and instruction.

Innocence is a wonderful thing—too bad it is so vulnerable, so **[405]** easily misguided. This is why even wisdom—usually concerned more with doing and not-doing than with knowing—also needs science; not so that we may learn anything from it, but so that our wisdom may gain some measure of acceptance and continuity for what it prescribes. We feel in ourselves a mighty counterweight to all the commands of duty so highly prized by reason—the counterweight presented by our needs and inclinations. Their combined satisfaction is called happiness.

Yet our reason urges its prescriptions unceasingly, without any concessions made to our inclinations. It ignores those urgent and seemingly reasonable claims that refuse to submit to any commandment. Out of this clash there emerges a *natural dialectic*, a tendency to split hairs over these strict laws of duty, thereby to cast doubt upon their validity, at least upon their purity and strictness. We want to make them conform, where possible, to our wishes and inclinations. We might want to corrupt them at their foundation and destroy their dignity—an outcome that would be unacceptable even to our common practical reasoning.

Thus *common sense* is driven to venture beyond its sphere and to take a step into the field of *practical philosophy*. It is driven not by any need for philosophical speculation (which leaves common sense alone, so long as it is content to remain that). Rather, it is driven to take this step for practical reasons. It seeks information and clear instructions to find the source of its own principle and its correct determination—in contrast to maxims based on nothing more than need and inclination.

Therefore, the aim of common sense is to escape embarrassment over competing claims and to avoid the danger of an ambiguity that may easily threaten all genuine moral principles. In becoming cultivated, practical reason gradually leads to a *dialectic* that compels it to look to philosophy for help. This dialectic occurs when we use practical as well as theoretical reasoning. Nowhere but in a complete critique of our reason will peace be found.

NOTES

[1] A *maxim* is the subjective principle of willing. The objective principle is that which would serve subjectively for all rational beings everywhere—to the extent that their desires are fully controlled by reason. This is law in practice, or practical law.

[2] One might object to my use of the word *respect*—as though I were merely trying to retreat into some obscure type of feeling, instead of giving a clear account of it by means of a concept of reason. Yet even if respect is a feeling, it is not *derived* from some external influence but is *created by ourselves* using a rational concept. It must therefore be distinguished from all feelings based on inclination or fear. What I directly recognize for myself as law, I recognize with respect. This simply means that my consciousness *subordinates* my will to law, without resorting to other influences on my senses. *Respect* means the direct determination of my will by law, and the consciousness of it. Such respect is seen as the *effect* of law on a person, and not as its *cause*. Respect for law is the idea of a value which dismantles my self-love. Thus it is to be seen neither as the object of inclination nor of fear, although it is analogous to both. The *object* of respect, therefore, is simply *law*—which we impose *on ourselves* and yet regard as necessarily valid in itself. Regarding it as law, we are subject to it, without any element of self-love coming into consideration. Regarding it as something imposed upon us by ourselves, it is a consequence of our will, so that in the first sense it is analogous to fear, in the second sense analogous to inclination. All respect for a person is but respect for law (for example, in respecting an honest person, we respect the honesty that person represents). When we recognize it as our duty to develop our talents, we also see in the talented person the example of a law that commands us to follow that example—and this expresses our respect. All so-called moral *interest* consists simply in the *respect* for law.

SECOND SECTION

Going from Popular Moral Philosophy to the Metaphysics of Morals

[406] Until now we have drawn our concept of duty from the ordinary way we use our practical reason. But let us not create the impression that we have treated it as a concept that arises from experience. Experience tells us something different. Considering how people act, we often hear the legitimate complaint that there has never been a sure example of an action arising from a pure sense of duty. Although some actions can *conform* to the dictates of *duty*, it seems that there never has been an action done *for the sake of duty* alone—and only on that basis can it have any moral worth.

Thus there have always been philosophers who have absolutely denied the sense of duty in human actions. Instead, all human motivation is put down to self-interest, more or less refined. Yet such philosophers have not succeeded in casting doubt upon the correctness of the concept of morality itself. What they have done, rather, is to express deeply felt regret at the fragility and impurity of human nature—which is noble enough to adopt the admirable idea of duty as a precept, yet too weak to follow it in action. Thus our reason, which ought to set up the law for us to follow, is used for nothing better than to see to the interest of our inclinations and try to make them agree with each other.

Indeed, it is simply impossible—by way of experience—[407] to establish with complete certainty a single case in which the principle of a dutiful action has rested entirely on moral grounds and on the demands of duty. Of course it often does happen that, after our most penetrating self-questioning in regard to a good action or a great sacrifice, we find that only the moral imperative of duty could have been powerful enough to move us to such acts. Yet despite this, we cannot rule out the possibility that our will was determined by some secret impulse of self-centeredness disguised as the idea of duty. We might flatter ourselves into claiming, falsely, a more noble motive for our actions. But even after rigorous self-questioning, we never can reach behind our hidden motivations completely—for in regard to moral worth, our concern is not with the actions we see, but with their inner principles, which we do not see.

There are those who will ridicule all morality as a mere phantom of human self-conceit seeking to outdo itself. We could hardly provide a more welcome service to them than to admit that the concept of duty must be derived entirely from experience (just as we like to convince ourselves, out of intellectual laziness, that this dependence on experience holds true for all other concepts as well). Then we give these moral skeptics a sure victory. Out of love for humanity, I will admit that most of our actions do accord with duty. But if we look more closely at our thoughts and efforts, we invariably meet up with the dear self, which is always there to provide us with a purpose for our actions—rather than the strict command of duty that would often require self-denial on our part.

As we advance in years and our power of judgment grows sharper with experience and observation, we may well come to doubt at times whether there ever is any genuine virtue to be met with in the world. To entertain such doubt, we need not be an enemy to virtue, but merely a cool-headed observer who does not confuse the liveliest wish with its realization.

If anything can guard us against the total deterioration of our idea of duty—if anything can help us sustain a well-grounded respect for the law of duty—it is this clear conviction: Even if there never were actions **[408]** springing from such pure sources, what really matters is not whether this or that action has occurred; rather, our reasoning power, independent of all appearances, commands what ought to occur.

This includes actions that have never yet been manifested in the world. Therefore, if we were to go by our experience alone, we might well doubt whether such virtuous actions are at all feasible. Even if there has never been a single example of a sincere friend, we would still be under the moral obligation to maintain pure sincerity in friendship. Even prior to all experience, this duty—as all duty in general—is implicit in the very idea of reason determining our will on *a priori* grounds, independent of experience.

So, if we are not to deprive the concept of morality of all truthfulness and all relation to some possible object, we must agree that the moral law must hold true not only for all human beings but for all *rational beings in general.* It must therefore hold true not under conditions of contingency and with exceptions, but it must count as a law that holds true out of *absolute necessity*. If so, then clearly no experience that is contingent could provide the basis for such necessary laws. If moral law were to be valid only in the contingent circumstances of humanity, how could we rightfully accord to it an unlimited respect as a universal principle for every rational being? And if these laws were empirical, based on experience—not fully *a priori*, nor having their source in pure practical reason—how could such laws, determining *our* will, be taken as laws determining the will of all other rational beings?

There could hardly be a worse foundation for morality than to suggest that it ought to be based on actual examples. The weakness in that approach is that every example that is presented must itself be judged beforehand according to moral principles—that is, judged to be worthy of serving as an example and a model for us to follow. Since it is dependent on more basic principles, there is no way that an example can provide the supreme concept of morality.

Even in the Gospels, the Holy One must first be compared to our ideal of moral perfection before he can be recognized. He says of himself: "Why do you call me—whom you can see—good? No one is the ideal of goodness, except God alone—and Him you do not see." **[409]**

But where did we get the concept of God as the highest good? Simply from the *idea* of moral perfection as constructed *a priori* by reason and linked inseparably to the concept of a free will. The realm of moral values has nothing whatever to do with imitation. Examples are of use only to encourage moral action—to show us that what is commanded by moral law is quite feasible and not to be doubted. Examples make visible what the rule of an action expresses in more general fashion. But examples cannot in themselves provide the *justification* for the example's original—for the moral commands originating from our reasoning—nor can we put the original principle aside and follow examples alone.

There is a truly supreme principle of morality, which rests entirely on pure reason and is independent of all experience. If there were no such supreme principle, I believe there would be no need to ask about the value of presenting these general concepts in abstract form. But there would still be some point in setting out these general concepts as holding true *a priori*, along with the principles associated with them—provided that the moral knowledge involved is to be distinguished from the ordinary kind of knowledge and is to be regarded as philosophical. However, in our own times it might be necessary to set out these general concepts; for if there were to be a vote to choose between a purely rational knowledge—separated from all empirical elements, as in a metaphysics of morals—and a popular practical philosophy, we can easily imagine which way the vote would go.

This descent into ordinary concepts is surely commendable, but only after the ascent to the principles of pure reason has been satisfactorily achieved. This would mean that the doctrine of morals must be given a metaphysical *foundation*. After being firmly established on that foundation, it must be given general *access*. But there is no sense in seeking popular support for the doctrine in the first instance, since the correctness of the fundamental principles depends on that foundation.

In any case such popular support would not bring it a genuine *philosophical popularity*. There is no great trick to being commonly intelligible if we give up the aim of achieving fundamental insights. Such an approach only brings out a shoddy mishmash of haphazard observations, randomly stuck together, along with principles that are only half reasoned. Empty heads enjoy this sort of thing; it provides the material for day-to-day chatter—while persons of discernment might feel confused by all this and turn their eyes away in dissatisfaction. Philosophers see through it all, but get little attention **[410]** in their effort to turn people away from such a falsely popular doctrine and towards genuine insight.

We need only look at the various attempts to relate to morality in the light of popular taste. At one time, people may regard morality as reflecting human nature (including the idea of a rational nature in general); at another time it may involve the idea of human perfectibility; or it may be seen to be directed at the goal of happiness; or it may be seen to be rooted in moral sentiment, or the fear of God—a little of this, a little of that, all in a wonderful mixture. But in all this we might forget to ask this question: Should the principles of morality be sought in our knowledge of human nature at all, that is, in a knowledge we can draw only from experience? Suppose that these moral principles cannot be found in human nature; suppose that they are completely *a priori* and free of everything empirical, conceived in absolute terms as derived from pure reason and from nothing else, not even in the smallest degree. Then our investigation ought to be conducted as something entirely separate from experience, that is, as a pure practical philosophy — or, to use that much abused phrase, as a pure metaphysics of morals.[1] In such a way, the investigation might achieve its final completion all by itself; and those who want what is popular will have to wait.

Such a completely insulated metaphysics of morals, then, is not mixed up with any element of anthropology or theology, physics or hyperphysics — still less with any occult qualities that could be called hypophysical. It is an indispensable foundation for all theoretical and truly definitive knowledge of duties, and, at the same time, a desire of the highest importance for the actual fulfillment of its precepts.

Thus the pure awareness of duty — untainted by any external admixture of empirical incentives or moral rules in general — takes the path of reasoning. By these means, reason first becomes aware that it can also become practical for itself. It has a far more powerful influence upon the human heart than all means of motivation[2] drawn from the empirical field. **[411]** With this awareness of its dignity, reason comes to despise such motivations and can gradually master them. On the other hand, a mixed moral philosophy moved by feelings and inclinations, and at the same time by rational concepts, makes the mind fluctuate between motives subject to no principle at all — so that the good is arrived at by mere chance and just as often as the bad.

What has been said so far shows:

- that all moral concepts have their source and basis entirely in *a priori* reason, and this, indeed, in the most common human reason as much as in the most highly speculative;
- that these moral concepts are not to be deduced from any empirical knowledge, and thus from anything merely contingent;
- that in this purity of their origin is their worthiness to serve us as the highest of practical principles;
- that to the extent that we add anything empirical in any given case, we deprive our actions of any genuine influence and of any absolute value;
- that it is of the greatest necessity, both in the speculative and in the practical sphere, that we create our concepts and laws out of pure reason, presenting them pure and unalloyed, and thus

determining in its full scope the complete capacity of this entire practical or purely rational knowledge.

Although speculative philosophy permits and often dictates [412] that we make our principles depend upon the particular nature of human reason, we ought not to follow suit. Rather, since moral laws must hold true for every rational being, these laws, in turn, must be derived from the universal concept of a rational being in general.

Though all morality, in its *application* to human beings, requires some knowledge of anthropology, the moral principles themselves must first be presented as being independent of all that is empirical, as pure philosophy, that is, as metaphysics. This can be done in the form of a separate investigation. Without possessing such a metaphysics, it would be useless to determine precisely, for speculative judgment, not only the morality of duty in everything that is done according to duty, but even in ordinary and practical use. This is especially true in moral instruction, where it would be impossible to establish morals on fundamental principles by trying to inculcate a moral disposition to achieve the highest good for humankind.

Although common moral judgment is quite worthy of respect, I will not proceed from such judgment to the philosophical, since this has already been done earlier in this work. Rather, I now proceed from a popular philosophy —which goes no further than it can by feeling its way blindly amidst examples—up to a metaphysics which is not limited by anything empirical. But since this must encompass the entire scope of rational knowledge, it advances to ideas where examples can no longer serve us. Thus we must proceed by natural stages to show clearly our capacity for practical reasoning, proceeding from the universal rules that determine it, to the point where the concept of duty arises from it.

Every single thing in nature works according to laws. Only a rational being has a *will*—namely the capacity to act *according to its own conception* of laws as principles. Since we need *reason* in order to base our actions on laws, the will is nothing but practical reason. If reason completely determines our will, the actions that are recognized as objectively necessary are also subjectively necessary. That is to say, the will is the capacity to choose *only* what is recognized by reason as being independent of any inclination, and to choose it as practically necessary, as good. But if reason, by itself, is not sufficient to determine the will, it still must be subject to other internal factors (for example, certain incentives) that do not always agree with objective factors. In a word, if the will *in itself* **[413]** is not fully in accord with reason (as is often the case in human beings), then our actions—although objectively recognized as necessary—actually are subjectively contingent. What determines such a will to accord with objective laws is *compulsion*. Accordingly, when our will is not thoroughly good, its relation to the objective goal is ascribed to the nature of rational beings. But due to its own nature, our will does not necessarily follow its own reasons.

The awareness of an objective principle, to the extent that it compels the will, is called a dictate of reason; the form of the dictate itself is called an *imperative*.

All imperatives are expressed in terms of the phrase "You *ought* . . . ." This demonstrates the relation of an objective law of reason to a will. In its subjective nature, such a will thereby remains necessarily undetermined (as in the case of compulsion). Imperatives say that it would be good to do or not to do something. But they address a will that does not always do something merely because we point out to it what would be good to do.

The practical *good*, however, is what determines the will by means of reason. Consequently, the will is guided not by subjective factors but by objective ones—by reasons that would be valid for every rational being. This must be distinguished from the merely *pleasant*, which exerts its influence on the will by means of sensations and other subjective factors and perhaps holds true for this or that individual, but not as a principle of reason valid for everyone.[3] **[414]** By the same token, a perfectly good will would come under the guidance of the objective laws (of the good). Still, this alone would not guarantee that a good will would make us act according to moral law. Rather, due to its subjective nature, the will is determined only by its own awareness of the good. Thus, for example, no imperatives hold true for a *divine* or a *holy* will. The moral *ought* is entirely out of place, here, since the *willing* is of itself necessarily in agreement with the law. Consequently, imperatives are only formulas for expressing the relation of objective laws of the will in general to the subjective imperfection of the will of this or that rational being, such as a human will.

In any *imperative*, the element of command is either *hypothetical* or it is *categorical*. It is a hypothetical imperative when we are aware of the practical necessity of a possible action as a means to attaining something else we might want. It is a categorical imperative when we are aware of an action as objectively necessary, without relating it to any other purpose.

Every law concerned with practice presents a possible action as good. Thus that action is presented as a necessary choice for any self-determining subject acting through reason. This means that all imperatives are formulas for determining an action according to the principle of choice made by a good will. Now if the action is only good as a means for achieving some *other* end, the imperative is *hypothetical*. If, however, the action is presented as good *in itself* and consequently as a necessary choice for a will that conforms to reason as its principle, the imperative is *categorical*.

Accordingly, the imperative says which of my possible actions would be good—by showing the practical rule in relation to a will that does not automatically do an action simply because it is good. This is so, in part, because the subject does not always know that the action is good; and in part, because even if it knew this, the ruling principle of the action could go against the objective principles of a practical reason.

Therefore, the hypothetical imperative merely says that the action is good for a *possible* or *actual* purpose. [415] The first is a *problematic* practical principle; the second is an *assertoric* practical principle. The categorical imperative declares an action to be objectively necessary in itself —without regard for any other purpose. In this sense it counts as an *apodictic* practical principle.

If we think of an action made possible through the powers of a rational being, we can also think of such an action as a possible goal for a will. Accordingly, the principles of action that are necessary for attaining an achievable goal are infinitely many.

All sciences have a practical part, consisting of problems indicating some goal attainable by us, and using imperatives that indicate just how that goal is to be attained. These can be called imperatives of *skill*. There is no question here as to whether the goal is rational and good; the question is only what we must do in order to attain that goal.

A doctor's prescriptions, intended to make a patient healthy, and the recipe of a poisoner, intended to kill a victim, are equal insofar as either one serves fully to achieve its purpose. Since we cannot know in our early years what goals may present themselves to us in later life, parents will seek to have their children learn *many different* kinds of things, taking care to develop in them *a variety of skills* in the use of means to *any sort of* ends. They have no way of knowing beforehand whether any given end will become an actual purpose in the child's life, although it remains a *possibility*. A parent is usually so concerned about such choices that there is no subsequent attempt on the part of the parent to justify or correct a specific choice or decision.

However, there is *one* such goal in life that we may definitely assume is shared by all rational beings—at least to the extent that they are contingent beings who allow imperatives to apply to themselves. We may assume a shared purpose that they not only *can* have but *do* have, by a natural necessity. This is the goal of *happiness*. When the hypothetical imperative shows the practical necessity of an action as a means for furthering the goal of happiness it is *assertoric*. In this, it is not to be regarded as being necessary towards an indefinite goal, one that is simply possible; rather, it is necessary towards a goal that can be prescribed *a priori* **[416]** for every person, as belonging to a person's very essence.

Choosing the means to promote our own greatest well-being involves an element of skill; let us call it *prudence* in the narrowest sense.[4] Thus the imperative regarding the choice of means towards our own happiness (in other words, the principle of prudence) remains *hypothetical*. The action is not commanded in an absolute sense but only as a means to another goal.

Finally, there is a categorical imperative. It has as its precondition that no purpose is to be served by it other than commanding an action unconditionally. This imperative is not concerned with the content of the action and its consequences. Rather, it is concerned only with the action's form and the principle from which it follows. What is essentially good in the action consists in the attitude involved, irrespective of what it accomplishes. This imperative may be called the imperative of *morality*.

In these three kinds of imperatives the act of willing is differentiated in *dissimilar* ways. To make the dissimilarity clear, I believe we can group them into *rules* of skill, *counsels* of prudence, and *commands* (laws) of morality. Only the concept of *law* carries with it an *unconditional necessity* that is objective and universally valid. Commands are laws that must be obeyed, even when they are contrary to our inclinations. *Counsel* also entails necessity, but only under subjective, contingent conditions. For example: Does this or that person count this or that element as contributing to happiness? The categorical imperative, on the other hand, is not limited by any precondition. It can quite properly be called a command, since it is necessary in an absolute, though practical, sense. One could also call the first group of imperatives *technical* (as belonging to art), the second group *pragmatic*[5] (as belonging to welfare) **[417]**, the third sort *moral* (as belonging to free conduct, that is, to morals).

Now the question arises: How are all these imperatives possible? We are not asking how we can carry out an action commanded by an imperative. Rather, the question aims to clarify just how the will is obligated when an imperative sets up an obligation. How an imperative *of skill* is possible requires no special clarification. In willing the goal, we also will the indispensably necessary means we possess toward achieving it (insofar as our reason has a decisive influence on our actions). This proposition is analytically true as concerns willing; for in my willing an object, as my effect, I have already thought of my causality as a cause, by thinking of the means to that object. From the concept of my willing this end, the imperative entails the concept of necessary actions to be taken toward this end. (To determine the means to some proposed end we need synthetic propositions, to be sure; but these are not concerned with the origin of the action, that is, the act of willing, but only with the problem of how to make its goal actual.)

For example, in order to divide a line into two equal parts I must draw, from its ends, two arcs that intersect. Mathematics teaches this by employing only synthetic propositions. But it is only through such an action that the desired effect can come about. To will the effect is to will the needed action as well. This is an analytic proposition. It is all the same whether I conceive of something as the effect of my action or conceive of myself as acting to bring it about.

If it were only that easy to form a definite concept of happiness, then the imperatives of prudence would be capable of giving us a definite concept of it, to which the imperatives of skill would conform perfectly, and thus they would be analytic as well.

In any case it could be said **[418]** that whoever wishes for a goal also wishes (as necessarily consistent with reason) for the sole means toward it within one's power. Yet it is unfortunate that the concept of happiness is so indefinite. Although every person desires to attain it, no one can say in a definite and consistent way just what it is one actually wishes and wants. This is so because all the elements belonging to the concept of happiness are, as a totality, empirical. That is to say, they must be borrowed from experience. But the idea of happiness requires an absolute totality, a maximum of well-being in our present and future condition.

Now it is impossible for any finite being — no matter how intelligent or well endowed — to form a definite concept of what we actually want. If what I want is wealth, then think of how much worry, envy, competition, and intrigue I have to face. Suppose I want knowledge and insight. It might give me only a sharper eye for detecting the evils now hidden from me, which though unavoidable now reveal themselves as all the more terrifying. Or it might yield more desires and thus intensify cravings that are already troublesome enough. Perhaps I wish for a long life. Yet who could guarantee that it would not be a lifelong misery? At least, perhaps, I want good health. Yet how often has our body's disability kept us from excesses we might have fallen into if we had been perfectly healthy, and so on!

In short, we are not able to determine precisely and with complete certainty on the basis of principle what would make us truly happy. Such certainty would need divine omniscience. In order to be happy, therefore, I cannot expect to act on the basis of definite principles, but only according to empirical advice. This might involve a proper diet, care with expenditures, good manners, decency, and so on (all the things that generally contribute the most to our well-being, as experience shows).

From this it follows that the imperatives of prudence, strictly speaking, cannot truly command. They cannot represent actions objectively as being *necessary* in a practical sense. They should be taken merely as wise counsel (*consilia*) rather than as precise dictates of reason (*praecepta*). To determine which action will promote the happiness of a rational being, with certainty and on a universal scale, is a problem utterly without a solution. There can be no imperative to tell us, in the strictest sense, what we must do to make ourselves happy. Happiness is an ideal set up not by reason but by imagination, resting entirely on empirical grounds. We would expect in vain **[419]** that they determine an action by which totality is achieved through an infinite series of consequences.

However, if we were to assume that the means to happiness could be stated with certainty, then the imperative of prudence would involve an analytic practical proposition.

In this way, the imperative of prudence would differ from the imperative of skill insofar as its aim is merely possible, while for the imperative of prudence the aim is given. But since both imperatives dictate the mere means to an already assumed end, and the means are already implicit in the end, both imperatives are analytic. Thereby, the imperative of prudence becomes possible as well.

On the other hand, we might ask: How is the imperative of *morality* possible at all? Undoubtedly, this is the only question demanding a solution, since this imperative is in no way hypothetical. The objective necessity presented by it cannot be supported by any presupposition (as is the case with hypothetical imperatives). But we must never lose sight of the fact that we can never demonstrate empirically—that is, *by means of example*—whether there is such an imperative. Rather, we must be aware that all imperatives that appear to be categorical might nevertheless be covertly hypothetical.

For example, someone might try to say: You must not promise deceitfully—and we assume thereby that the necessity of this prohibition is more than just a piece of advice for avoiding a further evil (as if to say: You must not deceitfully promise, so that your credibility will not be threatened if the truth is exposed). Rather, if we assert that an action of this sort is to be regarded as evil in and of itself, then the imperative of this prohibition is categorical.

Nevertheless, a mere example cannot prove with certainty that the will, in this case, is determined by the moral law alone, and by no other motivation, even if that may appear to be the case. For it is always possible that the will might covertly be influenced by a concern about possible disgrace, or some worry about other dangers. Who can prove by experience that there is no cause of an action, when experience shows only that a cause is not perceived? But in such a case, the so-called moral imperative—which appears categorical and unconditional—would in fact be only a pragmatic rule. It would simply draw our attention to whatever is to our advantage and teach us to keep it in view.

We will therefore have to determine the possibility of a *categorical* imperative entirely *a priori*. Since we do not have the advantage of experiencing the categorical imperative in its reality **[420]**, we would not need to establish that it is possible, but would only have to clarify it. This much can be seen so far: The categorical imperative alone can serve as a *law* of praxis; the rest, as a whole, may be called *principles* of the will, but not laws. This is so because whatever needs to be done to attain some arbitrary purpose may be seen as in itself contingent. We are free of the prescription for achieving a given purpose whenever we give up the purpose itself. On the other hand, the unconditional commandment does not allow the will to choose an opposite; only such an unconditional commandment has the required necessity a law demands.

It is difficult indeed to grasp this categorical imperative or law that governs moral action and to realize what makes it possible. The categorical imperative is a practical, synthetic *a priori* proposition. Such synthetic *a priori* propositions are difficult enough to fathom in *theoretical* knowledge, and are certainly no less so in practical knowledge.[6]

In approaching this problem, we want first to see whether the bare concept of a categorical imperative might not also provide the formula containing the one and only proposition that could actually be a categorical imperative. This investigation will involve special difficulties concerned with how such an absolute command is possible. These considerations we shall defer to the concluding section.

In thinking of a *hypothetical* imperative in general, I cannot know beforehand what it will entail until its precondition is stated. But if I think of a *categorical* imperative, I know immediately what it entails. Apart from the law, the categorical imperative entails only the necessity that the maxim[7] be in accord with the law. **[421]** The law itself, however, includes no precondition by which it is limited. What remains, therefore, is nothing but the universality of the law itself, to which the maxim of the action is to conform. It is this very conformity which the imperative represents as being necessary.

Accordingly, there is only one categorical imperative, and this is it: *Act only according to the maxim by which you can, at the same time, will that it should become a universal law.*

Now if, out of this one imperative as its principle, all imperatives of duty can be derived, it might be the case that the concept of duty still is an empty concept; yet with this one imperative alone we can still show what duty is and what we must mean by it.

Further, the universality of law, by which all effects occur, goes to make up what is called *nature*. In other words, the existence of things is determined by universal laws. This is according to its most general sense, namely, from the standpoint of form. With this in mind, the universal imperative of duty could be expressed as follows: *Act as if*

the maxim of your action were to become, through your
willing it, ***a universal law of nature****.*

Now let us enumerate some duties, according to the
conventional division between (1) duties to oneself and duties
to others, and (2) perfect and imperfect duties.[8]

EXAMPLES:

1. A man sinks into hopelessness after a series of
misfortunes, and feels sick of life. **[422]** He thinks of
committing suicide, yet he is still sufficiently in possession
of reason to ask himself whether this would not go counter
to his duty to himself. He wonders whether the maxim of his
contemplated action could serve as a universal law of nature.
His maxim is: "Out of self-love I make it my principle to
shorten my life, if its continuation threatens to bring me
more evil than good." It remains to be asked whether this
principle of self-love could become a universal law of nature.
But we soon see the contradiction. In any system of nature,
the feeling of self-love serves to promote life's continuation.
If that same feeling were to serve as the basis for destroying
your life, such a self-conflicting system could not possibly
persist. Nor could such a maxim hold as a universal law,
since it would go against the highest principle of duty.

2. Another man, in dire financial need, finds himself
pressed to borrow money. He knows perfectly well that he
will not be able to repay the debt. But he also sees that no
money would be lent to him unless he firmly promises to
repay at a specific time. He is tempted to make such a
promise; yet he has sufficient conscience to ask himself
whether it is not forbidden and contrary to duty to get out of
his difficulties in this way. Suppose he decides to do so; the
maxim of his action would be: "If I believe that I am in need
of money, then I shall borrow it and promise to repay,
although I know that this will never happen." Now this
principle of personal advantage may well be compatible with
his entire future well-being—but the overriding question is:
"Is it right to do this?" Here we transform the principle of
selfishness into a universal law, and restate the question as
follows: "What if the maxim were to become a universal
law?" We see immediately that the maxim could never serve
as a consistent law of nature, but that it must necessarily
contradict itself. A universal law stating that anyone who
believes himself to be in need can promise anything, without
any intention of repayment, would make promising

impossible, since no one would believe the promise, and would ridicule it as meaningless pretense.

3. A third man discovers in himself a talent that, were he to develop it, would make him **[423]** useful to society in many ways. But since he is in comfortable circumstances, he prefers to devote his life to the pursuit of pleasure, rather than taking the trouble to extend and improve his fortunate natural abilities. Yet he asks whether his maxim, apart from the consistency inherent in wasting his talents and enjoying his pleasures, is also consistent with duty. But now he realizes that a system of nature could indeed exist in accordance with such a universal law, by which he would allow his talents to decay and would apply himself to idleness, amusement, and procreation, that is, to a life of sheer enjoyment. Yet he cannot possibly *will* that this should become a universal law of nature or that such a law be part of our natural instinct; for as a rational being, he necessarily wishes for the development of all his faculties, since these are given and useful to him for all kinds of possible ends.

4. A fourth man is well off, but he sees others struggling against all sorts of hardships. He could easily help them, but he thinks: "Why should I be concerned with this? Let everyone be as happy as heaven wills, or as any person can be. I will take nothing from such people, nor even envy them. But I have no desire to contribute in any way to their well-being or to alleviate their need." If such a way of thinking were to become a universal law of nature, the human race might surely thrive, no doubt even better than with everyone prattling about sympathy and good will—sometimes trying to put it into practice. Yet we might cheat at times and betray or violate the rights of others. But although it is possible that a universal law of nature could subsist according to that maxim, it is nevertheless impossible to *will* that such a principle be taken as a law of nature; for such a will would contradict itself. There might be situations where I might need the love and sympathy of others, and where, by my own decree, I would deny myself all hope of the assistance I am looking for.

These are some of the many actual or presumed duties, **[424]** drawn from the single principle we have stated. We must *be able to will* that a maxim of our action should become a universal law. This is the canon for the moral evaluation of our actions. Some actions are such that their maxims cannot even be *thought of* as universal laws of nature—let alone be *willed* that it *should* be such. In other cases, the first impossibility is not to be found, but it might still be impossible to *will* that their maxim be raised to the universality of a law of nature without falling into contradiction.

From what has been said, we can easily see that the first maxim contradicts the strict or narrow sense of duty (where no exceptions are possible) while the second maxim contradicts only the broader (meritorious) duties. From these examples we can see how all duties with regard to their obligation (but not the goal of their action) are derived from one single principle.

If we really pay attention to what we are doing, we will find that in every violation of a duty we actually do not *will* that our maxim should become a universal law, since that is quite impossible. Rather, its opposite should remain a universal law. We reserve for ourselves the liberty of making an *exception* to the rule ("just this once") to serve our personal inclinations. Consequently, if we were to weigh everything from one and the same viewpoint, namely, that of reason, we would come upon a contradiction in our own will; namely, that a given principle is objectively necessary as a universal law, while subjectively it should not be universal but admit of exceptions. But since we regard a single action—now from the viewpoint of a will in accord with reason, now from the viewpoint of a will affected by personal inclination—there is actually no contradiction here. There is only the resistance   (*antagonismus*), of our inclination to accept the dictate of reason by which the character of the maxim is changed into a mere generalization (*universalitas*), so that the principle of practical reason might coexist with the maxim. Clearly this approach cannot be justified in our impartial judgment. Yet it indicates that we do accept the validity of the categorical imperative (with all due respect), while allowing ourselves a few minor and unavoidable exceptions.

[425] What we have shown so far amounts at least to this: If duty is a concept embracing the very meaning and actual legislative authority for our actions, it can be expressed only in terms of categorical imperatives and not at all in terms of hypothetical imperatives. At the same time, we have clearly presented the content of the categorical imperative as relevant to every application, and as containing the principle of all duty (if there is to be any such thing at

all). This is already no small feat. Yet we have not yet come so far as to demonstrate *a priori* that such an imperative actually exists. We did not yet show that there is a practical law that has the power to command absolutely, entirely of itself and without incentives, and that duty is the obedience to such a law.

With this purpose in mind, there is a warning we must take as being of the highest importance: We must not try to derive the reality of this principle from any *particular characteristic of human nature*. Rather, duty must be based on the practical unconditioned necessity of an action. Thus a duty must hold true for all rational beings (since only for them can an imperative be at all applicable), and *for this reason alone* can it be a law for human will. However, we could think of what might be traced to some particular human capacity, to certain feelings and inclinations, to a special tendency of human reason and is *not* necessarily valid for the will of every rational being. All this can indeed serve as the basis of a maxim for us, but not as a law. That is, this might lead to a subjective principle according to which we may act if we were so inclined. But it would not lead to an objective principle according to which we *are obliged* to act despite every opposing inclination and tendency. Indeed, the dignity and inner worth are much more evident in a command of duty, the smaller the role of its subjective causes. These opposing subjective factors do not in the least affect the necessity of a law, or diminish its validity.

Here we see philosophy placed on an uncertain footing, when its basis ought to be quite firm, even if there were nothing in heaven or on earth for it to base itself upon. Here philosophy ought to show its purity as the sole proprietor of its laws, not as the mouthpiece of a closed mind or an authoritative nature. Although these might well be better than nothing, they can never serve to establish principles dictated by reason. **[426]** Such principles must have their source entirely *a priori*, deriving nothing from human inclination, but everything from the supremacy of law and from what we owe to it. Without this, what remains but self-hatred and inner loathing?

Thus everything empirical is not only useless as an ingredient of moral principle; it is also extremely harmful to the integrity of morality itself. The genuine and exalted worth of an absolutely good will consists precisely in the fact that the principle of action is free of all contingent influences, which is the most that experience can provide. With all possible emphasis, therefore, we must warn against this careless and base mode of thinking that seeks its principle amidst empirical motives and laws. Human reason, when it grows weary, is only too glad to rest on this pillow. In its dreams of sweet illusions of morality, it substitutes a botched-up monstrosity—looking like anything one may wish, but not at all resembling true virtue in the eyes of someone who has glimpsed it in its true shape.[9]

The question, therefore, is this: Is it a necessary law *for all rational beings* that they always judge their actions according to maxims that they can will to serve as universal laws? If there is such a law, it must be connected (fully *a priori*) with the concept of the will of a rational being in general. But to discover this connection, we must (despite our resistance) take a step towards metaphysics, into an area of it that is different from speculative philosophy, namely, the metaphysics of morals. [427] In practical philosophy, we do not look for grounds to explain what *happens*, but rather for laws, that is, for objectively practical laws to determine what *ought to happen*, even if it never happens. Thus it is not necessary to embark upon an investigation as to why something pleases or displeases us; or how the pleasure of mere sensation differs from taste; or whether taste differs from a general satisfaction of reason; or what the feelings of pleasure and displeasure rest on; or how desires and inclinations arise from them; or how maxims arise from these, with the aid of reason. All this belongs to an empirical psychology that would constitute the second part of a science of nature—if, that is, it were regarded as a *philosophy of nature*, based on *empirical laws*. Here, however, we are concerned with objectively practical law, and consequently with the relation of a will with itself insofar as this is determined by reason alone. Then everything that is related to what is empirical falls away of itself, because if reason determines conduct *entirely on its own*, then it necessarily does this *a priori*. (We now turn to consider the possibility of such a determination.)

We think of the will as the ability to determine its own actions according to the awareness of certain laws. Such an ability can be found only in rational beings. In its activity of self-determination, the will is served by its objective ground—its *aim*, or *end*. An aim, when presented through reason alone, must be equally valid for all rational beings. What is called the *means* to an end contains only the possibility of an action, in its ground or source. The subjective ground of desire is the *incentive*; the objective ground of willing is the *motive*. This explains the difference between subjective ends, which rest on incentives, and objective ends, which rest on motives and are valid for every rational being. The principles of action are to be considered as *formal* if they abstract from all subjective ends; but they are *material* principles if they are based upon subjective ends, and consequently on certain incentives. As a rational being, we may arbitrarily set out for ourselves certain material aims as the *outcome* of our action. These are all merely relative; it is only their relation to a subject's specially constituted capacity for desire that gives them their worth. Therefore such individual worth cannot include any *universal* principles **[428]** valid and necessary as practical principles for all rational beings, and for every volition. Thus all these relative ends can serve only as grounds for hypothetical imperatives.

Let us assume that there were something whose *existence in and of itself* had absolute value—something which, as an *end in itself*, could be a ground for certain laws. In this, and in this alone, would be the ground of a possible categorical imperative, that is, a practical law.

Now I say that human beings, and in general every rational being, *exist* as ends in themselves, *not as mere means* for arbitrary use by another will. Rather, in all actions—whether directed at ourselves or other rational beings—we must *at the same time* and at all times be regarded *as an end.* All objects of inclination have only a conditional worth; for if there were no inclinations or needs based on them, their object would be without value. The inclinations themselves, however, as the sources of needs, are so lacking in absolute value that the universal wish of every rational being must be to free ourselves from them. Thus the value of every object that is *acquired* through dour action is always conditional. Those beings whose existence does not depend on our will but upon nature—if they are beings without reason—nevertheless have only a relative value, as a means, and are therefore called *things*, while rational beings are called *persons*. This is because persons are already distinguished as *ends in themselves*, as entities that are not to be used as mere means to an end. Therefore, their arbitrary exploitation is to be curtailed (and they are to be treated with respect). The point is that a person is not a merely subjective end, whose existence, seen as the effect of our action, has a value *for us*. Rather, a person is an *objective end*, one whose existence is an end in itself—one for which no other end can be substituted, as though the person were meant *merely* to serve it. If that were so, there would be nothing of *absolute value* outside it. But if all value were conditioned (and therefore contingent), then there would be no highest practical principle to satisfy reason.

If there is to be a highest practical principle, a categorical imperative for human will, then we must be aware of an aim that is necessary for everyone. Because it is an *end in itself* **[429]**, comprising an *objective* principle of will, it can serve as a universal practical law. The ground of this principle is this: *rational nature exists as an end in itself.* This is how we see our own existence, and to that extent it is a *subjective* principle of human action. But by the same token, every other rational being also sees its existence in this way—on the same rational basis that makes it applicable to me.[10] Therefore, it is simultaneously an *objective* principle, from which, as the highest practical ground, all laws of the will can be derived. The practical imperative will therefore read as follows: *Act in such a way that at all times you relate to humanity (whether it be in your own person or in the person of another) as an end, never as a mere means to an end.* Let us now go on to see whether this principle can be applied in practice.

We return to our previous examples:

First, concerning the concept of the necessary duty toward ourself, the individual contemplating suicide will ask whether such action can coexist with the idea of humanity *as an end in itself.* By doing away with myself in order to escape a situation that is too difficult to bear, I would make use of myself only as a *means* for maintaining a bearable situation till the end of my life. A human being, however, is not a thing, to be used *merely* as a means. Rather, in all actions and at all times human beings must be regarded as *ends in themselves.* Accordingly, I cannot treat humankind in my own person in such a way as either to mutilate, corrupt, or kill it. (There should be a more exact determination of this principle, so as to avoid all misunderstanding: for example, what about the amputation of a limb in order to save your life, or exposing yourself to danger in order to save your life, etc. But I will ignore all this, here, because it belongs to a discussion of morals proper.)

Second, in regard to a necessary or strict duty to others, the person who contemplates making a false promise to others will immediately see that this makes use of other persons *as mere means* to an end, without allowing them also to share in that end. The person I intend to use for my purposes cannot possibly concur with my action, **[430]** which is aimed against that person, and cannot embody the aim of this action. This creates a conflict with the principle of my duty to others, a conflict that becomes clearer if we take examples from attacks on the freedom or property of others. For then it is obvious that in violating the rights of others we intend to make use of those persons merely as a means to an end, without considering the fact that they—as rational beings—are to be regarded as ends in themselves. Only as beings who must at all times embody the goal of an action can they be truly valued.[11]

Third, in regard to contingent (meritorious) duty toward myself, it is not enough that the action should not conflict with humanity in our person as an end in itself; it must also be in *harmony* with that end. Now, there are in humanity as a whole certain capacities for our greater perfection; and nature can be said to have certain definite ends for those capacities—human ends that each of us may be expected to fulfill in our own person. We could easily neglect those ends and humanity would *survive* as an end in itself, but it would not *promote* that end.

Fourth, in regard to the meritorious duty we owe to others, the natural goal of all human beings is their happiness. Certainly, humanity would continue to exist if no one contributed to the happiness of others—as long as no one did anything purposefully to deprive them of it. This would be in harmony with the concept of *humanity as an end in itself;* but it would harmonize negatively, not positively, if each of us did nothing to promote the goals of others. If the idea is to have its full effect, then the ends of others, who are also ends in themselves, must as far as possible also be *my* ends.

This principle of humanity in general, and of every rational being *as an end in itself*—which is the highest limiting condition for the freedom of action in every person—is not derived from experience. **[431]** First, this is so because the principle is universal, meant to apply to all rational beings in general. There is no experience broad enough to determine any one thing about all of them. Second, we do not usually think of humanity as the goal for all (subjective) human beings. Humanity is not the goal we actually choose as our subjective end. Rather, it is an objective end that, as a law, embodies the highest limiting condition of all subjective ends, regardless of any other goals we might have. Therefore, it must originate from reason. The basis of all practical legislation lies *objectively in the rule* and in the form of universality that makes it capable of being a law, possibly a natural law (according to the first principle). But it lies *subjectively* in its *purpose*. The subject of all goals, however, is every rational being as an end in itself (according to the second principle). From this now follows the third practical principle of will as the highest condition of its harmony with universal practical reason, which is the idea of the *will of every rational being* as capable of *legislating a universal law*.

In line with this principle, we must reject all maxims that are in conflict with our own universal legislation of the will. Thus the will is not only subject to the law, but is so in such a way that it must also be regarded as *legislating for itself*.

For this reason above all, the will must be seen as subject to the law (and able to consider itself as the originator of it). The foregoing versions of the categorical imperative presented the general concept of the lawfulness of actions—a lawfulness resembling the lawful *order of nature*, or the general *purposefulness* of rational beings as ends in themselves. Due to the categorical nature of these imperatives, we excluded every element of personal interest as a motive, so as to insure in this way that these imperatives would be represented as truly categorical. However, they were only *assumed* to be categorical in order to enable us to clarify the concept of duty. Indeed, it would be impossible to prove that there could be such things as practical propositions capable of commanding categorically. Nor can it be done at this point in our discussion. One thing we could have proved is what it means to will on the basis of duty. Thus we would have rejected personal interest in such an act of willing as the element that differentiates the categorical from the hypothetical imperative. Something in the categorical imperative expresses this rejection. [432] This is found in the third formulation of the principle, namely, in the idea of the will of every rational being as a *universally legislating will*.

Such a will, being subject to laws, might well be linked to this law by some interest or other. Yet a will that is uppermost in the process of making laws cannot depend on any interest; for such a dependency would require a further law that would restrict its self-interest to the condition that it itself be valid as a universal law.

Let us assume that the above *principle* is correct: the will *of every individual is capable of legislating a universal law through all of its maxims.* In this case, it would accommodate itself easily enough to the categorical imperative *contained* in it, namely that it can command only if it is *based on no personal interest* for the sake of legislating universally. Among all other possible imperatives, it alone can be *unconditional*. Or, even better, let us turn the proposition around: if there is to be such a categorical imperative, a law that holds for every rational being, it can only command to do everything through the maxim of its own will, having itself as its object and thereby legislating universally. Only then is the practical principle, together with the imperative it obeys, unconditional, because it cannot have any personal interest as its basis.

There have been numerous efforts to make the basic principle of morality discernible. Looking back upon these efforts it is no wonder that they all had to fail. The individual person was seen to be bound by laws through the element of duty. But never did it occur to anyone to regard individuals as subject only to *their own* legislation and yet to a *universal legislation* or as bound to act only according to their own will, yet bound by the purposes of nature to act in accordance with a will that legislates universally; for if we think of individuals as subject to law (whatever it might be), the law **[433]** must carry with it some interest as incentive or compulsion. Thus the law did not spring from *their* will. Rather, the will was seen to be required by *something else* to act in a certain way. But as a result, all effort to find the highest justification of duty was irrecoverably lost. What was found was never the principle of duty, but only the need to act in the light of a certain interest. This could be one's own interest or the interest of someone else. But no matter what, the imperative always had to be conditional, contributing nothing in the way of an absolute moral command. Therefore, I will call this basic tenet the principle of the *autonomy* of the will, in contrast to the other, the *heteronomy* of the will.

This leads to the concept that every rational being must regard itself as universally legislating through all the maxims of its will, so as to judge itself and its actions from this viewpoint. This, in turn, leads to another very fruitful concept that is dependent on it—namely, that of a *realm of ends*.

By the term *realm*, I mean the systematic union of different rational beings through shared laws. Now, laws determine ends according to their universal validity. And if we abstract from the personal differences of rational beings and from all contents of their private ends, then we can think of a totality of ends. (This would include all rational beings as ends in themselves, as well as whatever personal goals they might individually set for themselves.) All these together would constitute a systematic whole, a realm of ends that would be possible by the foregoing principles.

Thus all rational beings are subject to the law by which individuals should treat themselves and all others *never as a mere means*, but always *at the same time as ends in themselves*. There arises, then, a systematic interconnection of rational beings through shared objective laws. Since these laws involve the interrelation of these beings as means and ends, the totality may be called a realm of ends (if only as an ideal).

But a being must be rational to belong to that realm as a *member,* both by legislating in universal terms and by being subject to these laws. And a rational being belongs to that realm as its *superior,* to the extent that in legislating it is not subject to the will of another. [**434**]

At all times, the rational being must regard itself as legislating in a realm of ends made possible through the freedom of the will, and as belonging to that realm as member or as superior. However, the place of the superior cannot be asserted through the maxims of will alone, but only if it is a fully independent being without need or limit with a capacity adequate to its will.

Accordingly, morality consists in the relation of all action to the process of making laws. Through this alone a realm of ends is possible. But this legislation must be present in every rational being, and it must be capable of arising from its will. The principle of that will, then, is this: never to carry out an action except on the maxim by which it can also be a universal law; and only such *that at the same time the will can regard itself as making a universal law on the basis of its maxim*. But what if the maxims, by their very nature, are not in a necessary accord with this objective principle, namely that rational beings are to be seen as universal legislators? According to that principle, the necessity of the action is called practical compulsion, that is, *duty*. In the realm of ends, duty is accorded not to the superior but to every member, and to an equal degree.

The practical necessity of acting in accordance with this principle of duty does not rest on feelings, impulses, or inclinations, but only on the relation of rational beings to one another. In this relation, the will of a rational being must always be regarded, at the same time, as *legislative*; otherwise it could not be thought of as an *end in itself*. Thus reason relates every maxim of the will as universally legislating to every other will and also to every action directed toward yourself. It does not do this for the sake of any practical motive or future advantage, but from the idea of the dignity of a rational being that obeys no law other than the one it simultaneously legislates for itself.

In the realm of ends everything has either a *price* or a *dignity*. Whatever has a price can be replaced by an *equivalent*; while whatever is above price has dignity.

Whatever is related to general human needs and inclinations has a *market price*. But there are things that do not satisfy a preset need and correspond merely to a specific taste, giving pleasure **[435]** to a merely purposeless play of our faculties. These things have what we may call an *affectional price*. In addition, there is something that comprises the precondition whereby something can have its purpose in itself alone. This does not have a relative value (that is, a price), but rather an intrinsic value, a *dignity*.

Now the only precondition for a rational being to be an end in itself is morality; for only in this way is it possible to be a legislating member of the realm of ends. Accordingly, only morality and humanity have dignity inasmuch as humanity is capable of morality. Skill and diligence in work have a market price. Wit, a lively imagination, and humor have an affectional price. On the other hand, such acts as keeping your promises and benevolence based on principle (not on mere instinct) have an intrinsic value. If these virtues are lacking, then nature and art can offer nothing to take their place. Their value does not consist in the effects arising from them, nor the advantage or utility they provide. Rather, the value of such virtues is in the attitudes connected to them, that is, in the maxims of the will that stand ready to be revealed in actions (even if the actions are not crowned with success). Further, in order for us to see them in a favorable light, these actions require no recommendation from any subjective disposition or taste, nor any immediate inclination or feeling. They simply present the will behind the actions, displaying the will as the object of immediate respect, which requires nothing more than reason in order to be *imposed on the will*. Nor should the will be lured into such actions, since this sort of talk contradicts the element of duty involved. This evaluation therefore enables us to admit the dignity of this way of thinking, placing it infinitely above all price. To bring it into comparison or competition with such a consideration would violate its sanctity.

What is it, then, that justifies the morally good attitude or virtue in making such lofty claims? It is nothing less than that share of the *universal legislation* it provides for a rational being. This makes a rational being fit to act according to its own nature as a member of a possible realm of ends. As an end in itself, it is thus entitled to legislate in the realm of ends and is free in regard to all laws of nature to obey only its own laws. According to those self-determined laws, a rational being's maxims can belong to universal legislation and, at the same time, allow for its subjugation to them. **[436]** For nothing else has a value but that which the law has determined for it. This legislation itself, however, determining all value, must for this reason possess a dignity, that is, an unconditional and incomparable value. As rational beings, we appropriately call it *respect*. Thus, *autonomy* is the basis for the dignity of human beings and of every rational being.

The three modes of presenting the principle of morality are formulations of the very same law; each formulation contains the other two. Nevertheless, there is a difference in them, which is more subjectively practical than objectively practical. The aim, here, is to bring an idea of reason closer to intuition (according to a certain analogy) and thereby closer to feeling. Thus all maxims have the following:

1) a *form*, consisting in universality, by which the formula of the moral imperative is expressed thus: that the maxims must be chosen as if they are to be taken as universal laws of nature;

2) a *matter*, namely an end, by which the formula states that a rational being, determined as an end by its very nature, and consequently as an end in itself, must serve in every maxim as a precondition limiting all merely relative and arbitrary ends;

3) a *complete determination*, with the formula: that all maxims stemming from our own legislation ought to harmonize with a possible realm of ends as a realm of nature.[12] A progression occurs here, as though the categories of the form of the will in its *unity* (by way of its *universality*) proceed to the *plurality* of matter (of objects, that is, goals) and thus to the *completeness* or totality of its system of ends. We do better, however, if in moral *judgment* we always follow the strict method by basing them on the universal formula of the categorical imperative: **[437]** *Act according to the maxim which can, at the same*

time, make itself into a universal law. But if we wish to win *acceptance* for the moral law, then it is useful to understand one and the same action in light of all three concepts and in that way bring the action as close to intuition as possible.

We can end at the point where we began, namely at the concept of an unconditionally good will. A will that is *absolutely* good is one that cannot be evil—which means that its maxim, when made into a universal law, can never contradict itself. This principle is therefore also its highest law: Always act according to the maxim whose universality as a law you can will at the same time. This is the only condition under which a given will can never conflict with itself, and such an imperative is categorical. There is an analogy between the validity of the will as a universal law for possible action and the universal connection of the existence of things according to universal laws as the formal aspect of nature in general. This link being understood, the categorical imperative can be expressed as follows: *Act in accordance with maxims that at the same time can have themselves as objects as universal laws of nature.* This gives us the formula of an absolutely good will.

Rational nature is distinct from other kinds of nature in that it sets up a goal for itself. This would be the material of every good will. But in the case of an absolutely good will, one without any qualifying conditions in its attainment of this or that end, we must abstract from every goal *to be attained* (since these would make every will merely relative to a given end). Thus we must think of the goal of a rational action not in terms of what it achieves but as existing *independently* of anything that would be achieved by it. Consequently, it must be thought of in a negative sense—that is, as an end that we must never act against and that we must never regard simply as a means but must respect at all times as an end that would be valued by every will. Now this goal can be nothing other than the subject of all possible goals themselves; for it is, at the same time, the subject of a possible absolutely good will, since this will cannot be subordinated to any other object without involving a contradiction. Accordingly, two principles are now shown to be fundamentally identical. The first of these says: Act in relation to every rational being (yourself and others) so that, at the same time, every rational being may count in your maxim as an end in itself. **[438]** The second principle says: Act according to a maxim that, at the same time, contains within itself its own universal validity for every rational being. In employing a means toward any end whatever, I must limit my maxims to the condition that they be universally valid as laws for everyone. A rational being must never be regarded as a mere means but as the highest limiting condition in the use of all means, that is, always and at the same time as an end. In other words: The subjective source of goals, the rational being itself, must provide the ground of all maxims of actions.

Now it follows indisputably from all this that every rational being must be able to see itself as an end in itself regarding all laws to which it may ever be subject, while, at the same time, legislating them on a universal scale. It is this very aptness of its maxims for universal legislation that marks it off as an end in itself. By the same token, this dignity (its prerogative), which sets it apart from all the mere things of nature, requires it, at all times, to see its maxims from its own perspective and from that of every other legislating rational being (who are therefore called persons). On this basis, a world of rational beings (*mundus intelligibilis*) is possible as a realm of ends, through the legislation on the part of all persons as members of this realm. Accordingly, every rational being must, at all times, act as if through its maxims it were a legislating member of the universal realm of ends. The formal principle underlying these maxims is this: Act as if your maxims were, at the same time, to serve as universal laws (of all rational beings). Thus a realm of ends is possible only on the analogy of a system of nature; yet the realm of ends is possible only according to maxims, that is, according to rules we have imposed on ourselves, while the system of nature is possible only in accordance with laws externally necessitated as efficient causes.

Putting such differences aside, we may call the totality of nature a realm of nature to the degree that it relates to rational beings as its ends, even though it might be seen as a mere machine. Such a realm of ends would actually be brought about by means of maxims that function as rules prescribing the categorical imperative for all rational beings—if such maxims *were to be universally obeyed*. But a rational being cannot count on such prompt universal obedience just because it strictly obeys the maxim itself. Nor can it expect that the realm of nature and its purposeful ordering harmonize with a rational being as a proper member of a realm of ends made possible through itself. That is to say, a rational being cannot necessarily expect that *its* pursuit of happiness be fulfilled. **[439]** Thus there is still the law which says: Act according to the maxims of a member who is legislating universally for a merely *possible* realm of ends. This law remains in full force because it commands categorically.

In this very point lies a paradox: On the one hand, the mere dignity of humanity as rational nature, without any other end or advantage to be gained—that is, the respect for a mere idea—should serve as an uncompromising prescription for the will. On the other hand, it is precisely this independence of the maxims from all such motives that should constitute their sublime character as well as the worthiness of every rational subject as a legislating member of the realm of ends. Without it, a rational being would simply be subject to the natural law that governs its needs.

But even if we were to regard the realm of nature and the realm of ends as united under one ruling principle—so that the realm of ends would no longer be simply an idea but would take on genuine reality—this would increase its motivation but not its intrinsic worth. For, in spite of everything, we would still need to picture an all-powerful lawgiver who would judge the worth of a rational being in light of the selfless conduct it prescribes for itself. So the essence of things is in no way changed by its outer relations. But apart from such considerations, whatever it is that constitutes the absolute value of a human being, on that alone it must be judged even by the Supreme Being. Thus, *morality* is the relation of actions to the autonomy of the will, that is, to a possible universal legislation by way of its maxims. An action is *acceptable* when it is compatible with the autonomy of the will; when it is not compatible, it is *unacceptable*. A will whose maxims necessarily agree with the laws of its autonomy, is a *holy*, absolutely good will. The dependence of a less than absolutely good will on the principle of autonomy (via moral compulsion), is moral *obligation*. Therefore, it cannot be related to a holy being. The objective necessity of an action done from obligation is called *duty*.

It is now easy to conclude how it all works: When we think of the concept of duty, we think of being subject to the law. At the same time, we associate a certain nobility **[440]** and *dignity* with individuals who fulfill their duties. These characteristics are absent insofar as we are *subjected* to the moral law; but they are present to the extent that we also legislate the law and are subject to it only by virtue of this act of legislation. We have also shown that neither fear nor inclination is the motive that gives an action moral value. Rather, the only motive that can bestow moral value on our action is simply our own respect for the law. The idea of our own will, made possible, is the true object of our respect, if it acts in accordance with its own universal maxims. Our dignity as human beings consists in this very capacity to legislate in universal terms, although under the condition of being, at the same time, subject to this very legislation.

The Autonomy of the Will as the Supreme Principle of Morality

Autonomy is that characteristic of the will through which it is a law to itself   (independent of all other characteristics of the objects of willing). The principle of autonomy says: Choose only in such a way that the maxims of your choice also include what you would want as a universal law. This practical rule is an imperative—namely, the will of every rational being is necessarily bound to the rule as a precondition. Because it is a synthetic proposition, it cannot be proven by means of the mere analysis of the foregoing concepts. We would have to go beyond the knowledge of objects to a critique of the subject, that is, of pure practical reason, since this synthetic proposition, which commands necessarily, must be capable of being known on an *a priori* basis; however, this concern does not belong in the present section. But that the principle of autonomy is the one and only principle of morals can be demonstrated quite well by the mere analysis of the concepts of morality; for by means of such analysis it is clear that the principle of morals must be a categorical imperative, commanding nothing more nor less than this very autonomy.

The Heteronomy of the Will as the Source of All Flawed Principles of Morality

[441] If the will were to look for its determining law anywhere else but in the fitness of its maxims to its own universal legislation; if the will were to go outside itself to study the character of any of its objects; then the result would always be *heteronomy*. In this case, it is not the will that gives law to itself; rather, the object does this by its relation to the will. This relation, whether it rests on my inclination or on the projections of my reasoning, allows only for hypothetical imperatives: I ought to do something *because I want something else*. By contrast, the moral,

categorical imperative says that I ought to do thus-and-so, even if I do not want something else. For example, the former says: I ought not to lie if I want to maintain my good name; the latter says, I ought not to lie, even if my reputation were not to suffer in the slightest. The moral point of view must therefore abstract from all objects or effects, so that they have no *influence* on the will. In this way, practical reason (or will) does not simply serve some interest outside it, but demonstrates its commanding authority as supreme legislation. Thus I ought to further the happiness of others, not because it touches me in some way (whether by an immediate inclination or by any satisfaction indirectly attained through reasoning), but only because the maxim that excludes it cannot be included in wanting it as a universal law.

Classification of All Possible Principles of Morality Derived from the Assumed Basic Concept of Heteronomy

Here as elsewhere, human reasoning, in its pure form and lacking critical perspective has tried all kinds of false paths before finding the true one.

All principles derivable from this viewpoint are either *empirical* or *rational*. Principles of the *first* sort, drawn from the principle of *happiness* [442] are built upon physical or moral feeling. Principles of the *second* sort are drawn from the principle of *perfection*, and are built either on the rational concept of perfection as the possible effect of our principles, or on the concept of an independent perfection (God's will) as a determining cause of our will.

Empirical principles are not at all suitable as a foundation for moral laws. The universality by which such principles should count as valid for all rational beings without exception—the unconditioned practical necessity imposed on them—falls away if the ground of such law is derived from the *particular arrangement of human nature* or from its contingent circumstances. The principle of *personal happiness* is the most questionable of all. It is false and, besides, experience contradicts the allegation that well-being is always proportional to good conduct. It is also questionable, because it contributes nothing to establishing a true basis for morality. Making someone happy is quite different from making someone good, just as making someone cleverly look out for his own advantage is quite different from making someone virtuous.

Rather, the pursuit of happiness attributes to morality incentives that undermine it, destroying its entire dignity. They place the motivation toward virtue in the same category as motivation toward vice, by teaching how to become more calculating, thus totally extinguishing the difference between virtue and vice. Yet the appeal to moral feeling remains, although superficially. Those who cannot *think* seek refuge in *feeling*, even when the question touches on universal law. But, the infinite spectrum of degrees of feeling is so subtle as to make it useless as a yardstick for good and evil; nor can we make valid judgments on the basis of our feelings for others.

Nevertheless, feeling — that supposedly special sense[13] — more closely resembles morality and its dignity; for it honors virtue, ascribing to it *directly* [443] the esteem in which it is held, without blatantly demonstrating that we appreciate morality not for its beauty but only for its advantage.

Among the *rational* grounds of morality, there is still the ontological concept of *perfection*. However, as a concept it is empty, indeterminate, and therefore useless in our attempt to find the right and greatest yield in the vast field of possible reality. In trying to grasp this reality, and in distinguishing it from every other, the concept of perfection exhibits an unavoidable tendency to turn around in circles by secretly presupposing the morality it is supposed to explain. Yet it is better than the theological concept of perfection, which seeks to derive morality from a most perfect divine will. The trouble is that we can have no direct experience of God's perfection but can only derive it from our own concepts, of which the concept of morality is the most prominent. In doing this (for if we did, it would get a circular explanation), we are forced to construct the concept of God's will from the characteristics of our own desire for honor and domination, combined with terrible images of power and vengeance, thus forming a system of morals totally opposite to morality.

But what if I had to choose between the concept of a moral sense and the concept of perfection? (At least neither one weakens morality, although neither one can serve in the least as its foundation.) I would choose the latter option, because the concept of perfection at least removes the question from the area of sense-experience and brings it to the court of pure reason. Although here, too, it does not decide, it nevertheless preserves the indeterminate idea (of a will that is good in itself), free of false elements for further investigation.

As for the rest, I believe that I might be excused for not presenting a lengthy refutation of all these doctrines. This would be easy to do, for even those who are committed to one theory or another (and whose audiences are intolerant of postponed judgments) would agree that the effort would amount to a waste of time. What is of greater interest to us here, however, is the knowledge that these principles can never set up anything other than heteronomy of the will; and for this very reason they must necessarily fail in the attempt.

Wherever an object of volition must be set out as a basis for **[444]** prescribing the rule that determines the will, the rule amounts to nothing but heteronomy. The imperative is then conditional, namely: *if* or *because* one wants this object, one ought to act in such-and-such a way, etc. Consequently, the imperative can never command in moral, categorical terms. The object may determine the will by means of inclination—for example, in connection with the principle of pursuing my own happiness, or by means of reason directed at an object of volition in general, as in connection with the principle of perfection. In such cases, the will never determines itself *directly* by means of the mental projection of an action, but only by means of the incentive that the anticipated action has upon the will: *I ought to do this, because I want something else.*

Here, a further law must be set in the subject, whereby I necessarily will the other thing, whose law in turn requires an imperative limiting this maxim. The impulse that makes the projection of the goal possible must work upon the will in accordance with the nature of the subject. This impulse belongs to the subject either through sensibility (such as inclination and taste) or through understanding and reason, which have it in their nature to derive pleasure from working on an object. Nature therefore provides the law that governs here. As a law that must be recognized and demonstrated through experience alone, it is contingent, not necessary. Consequently, it is not fit to serve as a rule of moral practice constituted by an apodictic practical rule. A law of nature, applied to morals, is *always mere heteronomy* of will. Such a will does not give itself the law; rather, an external impulse gives it the law, in accordance with the subject's natural readiness to receive it.

An absolutely good will—whose principle must be a categorical imperative—will therefore be indeterminate in regard to all objects, and will comprise only the *form of volition*. As autonomous, it will contain the fitness of the maxims of every good will to make themselves into the universal laws. This is the only law which the will of every rational being imposes upon itself—without relying on any incentive or interest as a basis.

How is such a synthetic a priori practical proposition possible? Why is it a necessary proposition? Answering these questions is a problem whose solution cannot be found within the borders of the metaphysics of morals.[445] Also, we have not asserted the truth of the proposition, much less pretended to be able to prove it. We were only able to show, by developing the universally popular concept of morality, that the autonomy of the will is inseparably bound up with it, being, indeed, its very foundation. Accordingly, whoever regards morality as something real and not merely a fanciful idea without truth, must simultaneously concur with our stated principle of morality.

This section, therefore, like the first, was merely analytic. We sought to show that morality is no mere fantasy; this must be so if the categorical imperative is true, together with the autonomy of the will—and that it is absolutely necessary as an *a priori* principle. To demonstrate this we must show that a *synthetic use of pure practical reason is possible*. Yet we must not venture into this area without preceding it with a critical examination of this very ability to reason. The final section will present the main lines of this *critique*, as far as is needed for our purpose.

NOTES

[1] Just as we distinguish pure mathematics from applied mathematics, and pure logic from applied logic, so we may distinguish a pure philosophy (metaphysics) of morals from its application to human nature. This designation immediately reminds us that the moral principles must not be based on the characteristics of human nature, but must subsist for themselves, *a priori*; and from such principles it must be possible to derive practical rules that hold true for every rational nature, and thus for human nature as well.

[2] I have a letter from the late and eminent J. G. Sulzer [1720–1779] in which he asks me: Why does the teaching of virtue achieve so little, though it is ever so convincing to reason? My reply (which was delayed by my wish to provide as complete an answer as possible) was that the teachers themselves have not clarified their concepts; they have looked everywhere for motivations toward moral goodness, but they spoil the medicine by making it too strong. The most common observation is that when we represent a righteous action done by a steadfast soul—apart from all considerations of advantage in this world or the next and apart from all temptations due to distress or enticement—it puts all similar actions to shame if they were done from some extraneous motive. Thus it uplifts the soul, and engenders the wish to be able to act in this way. Even children, in their middle years, feel this impact, and duties ought not to be represented to them in any other manner.

[3] When desire is dependent on sensations it is called inclination, and this always indicates a *need*. Now consider a contingently determinable will. When such a will is dependent on principles of reason, it is an *interest*. This occurs only in a dependent will, which is not always in accord with reason. Thus we cannot imagine God's will as having an interest. But the human will can *take an interest*, without necessarily acting *out of interest*. The first of these signifies the *practical* interest in an action; the second signifies the *pathological* interest in the object of the action. The former indicates only the dependence of the will on principles of reason in themselves; the latter indicates the dependence of the will for the purpose of inclination—since reason specifies only the practical rule whereby the needs of inclination are satisfied. In the first case, what interests me is the action; in the second case the object of the action (so far as it is pleasant for me). In the first section we saw that when an action is done from duty we must not consider the interest in the object, but only the action itself, and its principle in reason (the law).

[4] The word "prudence" is understood in a twofold sense: in one sense it is taken as "worldly wisdom," in another sense as private wisdom. The first of these involves a person's skill in influencing others to serve one's own ends; the second is the ability to combine these purposes towards one's own permanent advantage. The latter is what the value of the former is based upon. And if someone succeeds in the first of these but not in the second, it would be more accurate to say such a person is shrewd and crafty but all in all is not wise.

[5] In my view, the real meaning of the word "pragmatic" could thereby be defined most precisely. We call pragmatic those *sanctions* that flow not from the rights of states as necessary laws, but out of the *provision* for the general well-being of a community. A *history* is written pragmatically if it teaches us to be *prudent*, instructing the world how it may best pursue its advantage, or at least as well as earlier times might have done.

[6] Without presupposing a precondition derived from an inclination of any sort, I venture to link—*a priori*—and therefore with necessity, the act with the will that motivated it. The connection is to be seen in an objective sense, i.e. under the idea of reason, which reigns over all subjective motivation. This is therefore a practical proposition which does not analytically derive the willing of an action from some other act of willing already presupposed (for we do not possess such a perfect will); rather, it is linked to the concept of the will of a rational being as something that is not analytically included in this concept.

[7] A *maxim* is a moral principle of action, seen from the *subjective* side. As such, we must distinguish it from the *objective principle*, i.e. the practical law. A maxim involves the practical rule determined by reason as

conforming to the conditions of the subject (including possible ignorance as well as personal inclinations). Thus it is the very principle according to which the subject *does act*. The law, however, as the objective principle, is valid for every rational being, and it is the principle according to which every rational being *ought* to act, i.e. an imperative.

[8] I reserve the division of duties for a forthcoming book, the *Metaphysics of Morals*. The present division is entirely arbitrary, for the sole purpose of giving order to my examples. By a "perfect duty" I understand a duty that admits of no exceptions in the interests of our inclinations. I therefore have not only outer *perfect* duties, but also inner *perfect* duties. This goes against the conventional usage adopted in schools—but I need not justify the division here, since it makes no difference whether it is acceptable or not.

[9] To glimpse virtue in its actual form involves nothing other than the presentation of morality stripped of all contamination by anything sensuous and all false adornment of reward or self-love. Then pure virtue must overshadow everything else that is attractive to one's inclinations. Anyone making the slightest effort of reasoning can see this, if reason is not yet totally corrupted for all abstract thinking.

[10] I introduce this proposition here as a postulate. The grounds for it will be presented in the last section of this book.

[11] We must not think, here, that the trivial formula, "Do not do to others what you do not want done to you," can serve us as a standard or a guiding principle. For if it is derived from our principle at all, it is only with various limitations that it is so. It cannot be a universal law, for it does not contain the ground of duties toward oneself, nor the duties of love toward others (since many a person would agree not to expect benefits from others, if only he were not obligated to extend benefits to them in return). Nor does the formula contain strict duties towards others—for on this basis, the criminal could take issue with the judge who pronounces sentence upon him, etc.

[12] Teleology considers nature as a realm of ends; morality regards a possible realm of ends as a realm of nature. In nature the realm of ends is a theoretical idea toward the explanation of what there is. In morality it is a practical idea for the purpose of making real what does not yet exist but can be made real by our activity, thus actualizing it according to this very idea.

[13] I count the principle of moral feeling to be close to that of happiness, since every empirical interest does contribute to our well-being, whether through something immediate, without advantage for us, or by reference to personal advantage. With Francis Hutcheson [1694–1746], we must accept the principle of empathy with the happiness of others, as belonging to the moral sense he set forth.

Going from the Metaphysics of Morals to a Critique of Pure Practical Reason

[446] The Concept of Freedom is the Key to Explaining
the Autonomy of the Will

Will is a form of causality of living beings that are rational; *freedom* is the particular quality of this causality that activates it, independent of external causes *determining* it. *Natural necessity* is a quality of the causality of beings that lack reason, determining their activity through the influence of external causes.

However, this explanation of freedom is *negative,* useless for investigating its essence. Yet, a *positive* concept emerges from it, far richer and more fruitful. Since the concept of causality entails the concept of *laws*—by which something called a cause is followed by something else, its effect—freedom is not entirely without laws, even though it is not simply an attribute of the will in accordance with the laws of nature. Rather, freedom involves a causality according to immutable laws, but laws of a special kind. Otherwise a free will would be nothing at all.

We have seen that natural necessity involves a heteronomy of efficient causes. Every effect is possible only according to a law **[447]** by which something else determines the effectiveness of its causality. What else can freedom of will be, if not the autonomy of the will, the quality of the will that is a law to itself? The proposition "In all actions, the will is a law to itself," expresses only the principle of acting according to no other maxim but that by which it can also have itself as the object of a universal law. This is the formula of the categorical imperative, the principle of morality. A free will and a will that is subject to moral laws are one and the same.

If we suppose that the will is free, morality must follow from it through the mere analysis of the concept of freedom. This is always a synthetic proposition. It says that an absolutely good will is one whose maxim can at all times include itself when it is seen as a universal law. But this quality of the maxim cannot be discovered by analyzing the concept of an absolutely good will. Rather, such synthetic propositions are possible only because both insights are linked to each other by their connection to a third, in which both are found. The *positive* concept of freedom provides this third quality. Unlike physical objects, this third quality cannot be the nature of the sensory world (in which the concept of cause involves a relation to something different as effect). We cannot directly demonstrate this third quality, the one to which freedom points us and of which we have an idea *a priori*. Nor can we, at this point, make comprehensible the deduction of the concept of freedom from pure practical reason, together with the possibility of a categorical imperative. For this, we need some further preparatory remarks.

Freedom Must Be Presupposed as a Quality of the Will of All Rational Beings

It is not enough to attribute freedom to our own will, on whatever grounds, if we don't also have adequate grounds for ascribing it to every rational being. If morality can serve as a law for us, as *rational* beings, this is because it serves as a law for all rational beings. Since morality must be drawn from the quality of freedom, we must prove that freedom is a quality of the will of all rational beings. **[448]** Further, it is not enough to present the idea of freedom from some supposed experiences of human nature. (Such proof is absolutely impossible and can be done only on an *a priori* basis). Rather, we must prove it as necessarily belonging to the activity of all rational beings that possess a will.

From a practical standpoint, every being incapable of acting other than under the idea of *freedom* is for that very reason truly free. All laws that are inseparably connected to freedom must be valid for such a being—just as if its will were proven by means of theoretical philosophy to be free in itself.[1]

We necessarily attribute the idea of freedom to every rational being that has a will; for only under this idea can such a being be understood to *act*. In such a being we think of practical reason, which means that it stands in a *causal* relation to its mental objects. It is impossible to imagine that such reasoning, being conscious of its own goals, would be directed by something external in making its judgments. The subject would not be able to ascribe the impetus to its power of judgment but rather to an impulse. Reason must see itself as the originator of its own principles, independent of any external influences. So it must see itself as free—whether as practical reason or as the will of a rational being. The will can be a will on its own only under the idea of freedom, which is why, in practical terms, such a will must be ascribed to all rational beings.

Regarding the Element of Interest Attached to the Ideas of Morality

We have taken the definite concept of morality back to the idea of freedom. Yet we could not prove that freedom exists as something real in ourselves and in human nature. [449] We saw only that we must presuppose it if we want to think of a being as rational, conscious of its own causality in regard to its actions, possessing a will. And so we find that on the very same grounds, we must ascribe to every being endowed with reason and will this attribute of self-determination under the idea of its own freedom.

However, from the presupposition of these ideas also followed the awareness of lawful action. The subjective principles of action, the maxims, must at all times be seen in such a way that they are also objectively valid as universal principles. Thus they may serve our own universal legislation. But why should I make myself subject to this principle, as a rational being, along with all other beings endowed with reason? No interest *drives* me to this, since this would not give me a categorical imperative. Yet I must *take* an interest in all this and see how it comes about, since "I ought" is actually "I will," valid for every rational being, as long as my reason is translated into practice without hindrance. Beings like ourselves are affected by other motives, such as sensuality. Things do not always happen according to pure reason; the necessity of action is dictated only by the ought so that the subjective necessity is distinguished from objective necessity.

It may seem as though, in the idea of freedom, we have actually presupposed the moral law, the principle of the autonomy of the will itself, as though we could give no proof of its reality and its objective necessity on its own. But even if this were so, we would still have gained something considerable. The genuine principle of morality would have been given a more exact determination than we usually achieve. But in regard to its validity and the practical necessity of subjecting myself to it, nothing further would have been achieved. Suppose someone were to ask us why the limiting condition of our actions must be the universal validity of maxims taken as a law; suppose we were asked about the ground of the value we give to this way of acting—this value being so great that there can be no higher interest involved. And why is it that human beings believe in their personal worth only on this basis, [450] so that their pleasant or unpleasant condition means nothing by comparison? We could give no satisfactory answer.

We can take an interest in someone's personal quality—even if this involves no interest in that person's condition, so long as the quality allows us to take part when reason determines its distribution. Thus I can appreciate someone's worthiness of being happy, even without taking part in it. But this judgment is only the result of moral laws whose importance we have already presupposed (provided we detach ourselves from all empirical interest through the idea of freedom). Now we cannot say, as yet, just why we should detach ourselves from our interest so that we may consider ourselves free to act although subject to certain laws. Presumably this stance enables us to find value in our own person, so that we are compensated for losing what gives value to our condition. On this basis, however, we cannot yet see how this is possible, or *how the moral law obligates us*.

We see a kind of circle from which, it seems, we cannot escape—we must freely admit this. In the order of efficient causes, we assume that we are free so that we may think of ourselves as subject to moral laws in the order of ends. Then we think of ourselves as subject to such laws because of our free will. Both freedom and the will's self-legislation constitute our autonomy; they are therefore reciprocal concepts—which is why we cannot use one of them to explain the other nor to provide the ground for the other. At best, we can use one of them, purely for the purpose of logic, to bring apparently different ideas of the same object under one concept (as we reduce fractions to their lowest common denominator).

However, there is a way out. We can separate the areas of inquiry, both thinking of ourselves as free causes and seeing our actions as themselves the effects of causes.

It does not take much subtlety to grasp this thought. It is obvious to the most common way of understanding by means of that oblique power of judgment, called feeling, which is that all awareness **[451]** that comes to us without our willing it (such as that from the senses) enables us to know objects only by how they affect us. How they are in themselves remains unknown to us. Even if we give them our closest scrutiny, with the greatest clarity reason can muster, all we can know of things is their *appearances*, never the *things themselves*.

Once we set up this distinction, we must necessarily admit that behind the appearances there is something that is not appearance, namely the things themselves. (Possibly we have only observed the difference between the awareness of things coming to us from outside ourselves, to which we are passively receptive, and the awareness we bring from within us, reflecting our activity of creating it.) We have to admit that we can never approach the things themselves directly, but only their appearances as they affect us; and that in trying to know them we can never get closer to them and can never know them as they are in themselves.

This leads to a division, however crude it may be, between *the world of the senses* and *the world of the mind*. The senses can vary significantly with the different sensuality of various observers; the mind, providing the ground of the former, always remains the same. We cannot even pretend to know ourselves by means of the inner sensation we have of ourselves. Since we do not create ourselves, and since we must get our self-concept not *a priori* but empirically, it is natural that only through our inner senses, only through the appearance of our nature and the way it affects our consciousness, can we attain knowledge of ourselves.

Although we have put together what we know of ourselves entirely from appearances, each one of us must realize that there is something more, namely our self, however it is constituted. Thus, to the degree that we have constructed our self-image by means of our awareness and sensations, we must be regarded as belonging to *the world of the senses*; yet, to the degree that all this comes down to our unmediated activity (not affected by the senses but arising directly from our consciousness) we must regard ourselves as belonging to *the world of the mind*, although we can get no farther into it than this.

Any reflective person must arrive at a similar conclusion regarding all the things that arise from consciousness. **[452]** Presumably, such a conclusion is also found in common understanding, with its inclination to expect that behind all sense-objects there is something unseen, operating alone—although such common understanding wants what it cannot have, which is to make it sensory and see what is invisible, so that, in the end, it is no wiser than before.

Now we find in ourselves the power to distinguish ourselves from all other things, even from ourselves, insofar as we are affected by anything external. This power is *reason*. As something unmediated and self-activating, reason is elevated even above our mind. Surely, our mind is also independent. Unlike the senses, it does not merely contain images that arise whenever we are affected by something external (to which we are passively receptive). And yet, however active our mind may be, it can create no concepts other than those that *place sensory ideas under rules*, thus uniting them in our consciousness. Without this activity, our mind could not think at all. On the other hand, we see that reason, under the name of ideas, exhibits such a pure spontaneity that it goes beyond anything that might be presented by the senses. Its highest task is to distinguish the world of sensation from the world of the mind. But it also shows the limits of the mind.

For this reason, as rational beings, we must consider ourselves to be *intelligent beings*—seen not from the aspect of our lower powers, not as belonging to the sensory world, but to the world of the mind. Accordingly, there are two possible points of view from which we can see ourselves and recognize the laws governing the use of our powers and thus all of our actions. *First*, insofar as we belong to the world of sensation, we see ourselves subject to the laws of nature (of *heteronomy*). *Second*, we see ourselves belonging to the intelligible world, subject to laws that are independent of nature, not empirical but grounded in reason alone.

As rational beings, and consequently as belonging to the intelligible world, we can never think of the causality governing our own will except as pertaining to the idea of freedom. Thus, our independence from the determining causes of the sensory world is freedom (and reason must always associate itself with that freedom). Inseparably tied to the idea of freedom is the concept of *autonomy*. To this is tied the universal principle of morality. This, in turn, is the ground of all actions of *rational* beings **[453]**, just as natural law is the basis of all things appearing in nature.

With this conclusion we have eliminated the earlier suspicion that it might contain a hidden circularity, as we go from the idea of freedom to autonomy, and from there to moral law. It seemed that we found grounds for the idea of freedom for the sake of the moral law, so that we might infer that law from the idea of freedom. This would mean that the moral law itself would have no real ground of its own, and that we only begged the question whether there was such a principle. One might well grant us this, but we could never demonstrate it as a valid proposition. But now we see something else. In thinking of ourselves as free, we think of ourselves as members of the intelligible world; we recognize the autonomy of the will along with morality as its consequence. But in thinking of ourselves as morally obligated, we regard ourselves as belonging to the world of the senses and at the same time to the world of the mind.

How is a Categorical Imperative Possible?

As a rational being, I count myself as belonging to the world of the mind. Only by regarding myself as an effective cause in that world do I call my causality a *will*. On the other hand, I am also conscious of myself as part of the sensory world; and here my actions are seen as mere appearances of that causality. Yet my actions cannot be seen to result from a mysterious causality that I do not know; instead, these actions of mine, as part of the sensory world, must be seen as resulting from other appearances—namely, desires and inclinations.

Accordingly, if I were only a member of the world of the mind, all my actions would conform perfectly to the principle of the autonomy of a pure will; and if I were only a part of the sensory world, my actions would conform entirely to the natural law of desires and inclinations—that is, to the heteronomy of nature. (According to the first of these alternatives, my actions would rest entirely on the highest principle of morality; according to the second alternative, my actions would rest on the principle of happiness.)

But the world of the mind also comprises the ground of the sensory world, and consequently its laws. Thus, with regard to my will (which belongs entirely to the world of the mind), the mind is its direct authority and must be thought of as such. **[454]** On the one hand I belong to the sensory world; on the other hand, I am an intelligent being and must recognize myself as belonging to the world of the mind. Therefore, I am subject to its laws, that is, to reason whose laws comprise the idea of freedom. I must see myself as subject to the autonomy of the will. Consequently, I must regard the laws of the world of the mind as imperatives for me and the actions corresponding to this principle as duties.

In this way, the categorical imperative is possible, because the idea of freedom makes me a member of an intelligible world. Now if I were only a member of that world, my actions *would* at all times conform to my autonomous will. But since I see myself, at the same time, as a member of the sensory world, my actions *ought* to conform to my autonomous will. This *categorical* "ought" represents a synthetic *a priori* proposition. Added to my will that is affected by my sensory desires is the idea of a will belonging to the world of the mind. This is the idea of a pure will that is active for itself. It contains the supreme condition of that will connected to reason. This is similar to the way in which concepts of the mind are added to our experience of the sensory world. In and of themselves these concepts mean nothing other than the form of law in general, making possible synthetic *a priori* propositions upon which all our knowledge of nature rests.

Practical human reasoning supports this deduction. Assume for a moment that we were to give someone examples of personal traits such as integrity of purpose and resoluteness in adhering to worthy principles, along with sympathy and general benevolence (even at the great cost of giving up personal advantages and comfort). Even the worst criminals would wish to have these traits, once they were displayed to them, provided that they are accustomed to using reason. Perhaps they cannot acquire these traits, if only because of their own inclinations and impulses; at the same time, they must surely wish to be rid of such burdensome inclinations. In this way, they prove that, with a will that is free of sensual impulses, they can intellectually transport themselves into an altogether different order of things, away from the realm of their sensual desires.

But the wish would not, by itself, satisfy the criminals' desires, nor would it produce any condition that would satisfy any of their genuine or conceivable inclinations (for then the idea that elicits the wish would lose its superior status). Instead, the criminals would have to admit that, as persons, they have greater inner worth than they had previously believed. **[455]**

Thus they believe that they can be better persons when they think of themselves as members of the world of the mind. The very idea of freedom, independence from the *determining* causes of the world of the senses, compels this. The consciousness of a good will within themselves constitutes the law whose authority they tacitly acknowledge, even as they transgress it. Therefore, as members of an intelligible world, the obligation of a moral "I ought" would necessarily become "I will." But as simultaneous members of the world of the senses, the obligation is only perceived as an ought.

Regarding the Ultimate Boundary of All Practical Philosophy

We all think of ourselves as free in regard to our will. This is why we make judgments about actions we *ought to have done*, even though they *were not done*. And yet, this freedom is not a concept derived from experience, nor can it be, because it remains forever. This is true in spite of the fact that our experience shows us the opposite of the demands we see as necessary for such freedom. On the other hand, it is equally necessary that everything that happens should, without exception, be determined according to the laws of nature. This natural necessity, too, is not a concept drawn from experience, precisely because it entails the concept of necessity, and along with it *a priori* knowledge. Yet the concept of nature is verified through experience and must be presupposed to be indispensible if experience is to be at all possible as coherent knowledge of sensory objects operating together according to universal laws. So, freedom is merely an *idea* of reason whose objective reality is in itself questionable; nature, on the other hand, is a *concept of the mind* which demonstrates its reality (and necessarily must demonstrate it) by means of examples drawn from experience.

From all this, a dialectic of reasoning arises in which the freedom we ascribe to the will seems to contradict the necessity of nature. At this parting of the ways, reason, with its speculative purposes, finds the path of nature's necessity easier and more useful than that of freedom. For *practical purposes*, however, the path of freedom is the only one enabling us to apply reason to our conduct. [**456**] Accordingly, it is just as impossible for the most subtle as for the most common form of human reasoning to argue its way out of freedom. So we must assume that there is no genuine contradiction between freedom and natural necessity in the very same actions since we can neither give up the concept of nature nor that of freedom.

But even if we could never comprehend how this freedom is possible, this seeming contradiction must be removed. If the thought of freedom—or the thought of nature, which is just as necessary—contradicts itself, then freedom would have to be completely given up in favor of natural necessity.

This contradiction would be inescapable if, in relation to any given action of mine, I were to think of myself and call myself both free and subject to the law of nature, *taking these in the same sense and relationship.* It is an unavoidable task of speculative philosophy at least to show that its error about the contradiction stems from the fact that, when we say a human being is free, it is in an altogether different sense from the way we think human beings as a part of nature and subject to nature's laws. In other words, speculative philosophy must show, not only that the two views *can* coexist quite comfortably, but that they must be regarded as *necessarily united* in any one person. Otherwise it would be impossible to explain why we must burden our reasoning with an idea which—although it can be united *without contradiction* with another well-proved idea—places our theoretical reasoning in a disadvantageous position. This is a duty only for speculative philosophy as it clears the way for practical philosophy. But we should not leave it to the arbitrary preference of the philosopher whether to confront this seeming contradiction or leave it alone. If we do, fatalism could easily enter this abandoned property and justifiably evict all morality as a squatter without legal title.

We could not say that the boundary of practical philosophy begins here, since the resolution of the conflict does not at all belong to the realm of practical philosophy. Rather, it demands of speculative reason only that it bring to an end [457] the disharmony by which it has involved itself in theoretical questions. Thus, practical reason may achieve peace and security from external attacks that would put into dispute the very ground on which it may want to build.

But the just claim to freedom of the will, as set out even by common human reasoning, bases itself on the consciousness and the admitted presupposition of reason's independence of subjectively determining causes. Together they constitute mere sensation and what comes under the general heading of sensibility. By such means, a human being regards itself as an intelligent being and places itself in a different order of things, thinking of itself as an intelligent being, endowed with a will and thus with causality. When considered as a phenomenon of the sensory world (which it also truly is), it perceives itself and its causality as subject to the external determinants of the laws of nature. Soon we become aware that both internal and external factors are valid at the same time, and that indeed they must be so. For there is not the slightest contradiction in saying that *a thing appearing in the sensory world* (and as belonging to that world) is subject to certain laws, while it is yet independent of such laws as *a thing or being in itself.* That we must think of ourselves in this dual way rests, first, on the consciousness that we can see ourselves as objects affected by sensation; and second, on our consciousness of ourselves as intelligent beings, as independent of sense-impressions whenever we use reason (and therefore as part of the world of the mind).

We attribute to ourselves an ability of will that ascribes nothing to our desires and inclinations alone. On the contrary, we think of actions as possible, even as necessary, when we can set all sensory stimuli aside. The causality of such actions lies within us as intelligent beings and in the laws of the effects and actions that happen according to the principles of the intelligible world. We know nothing about such a world, other than the fact that, in it, reason alone—reason independent of sensibility—provides the law. In view of the fact that we are our actual self only as intelligent beings (while seeing ourselves only as an appearance), these laws apply to us directly and categorically.

As a consequence, the incitements that result from inclinations and impulses (and from the entire world of sensory nature) cannot hinder our willing as intelligent beings. **[458]** We do not even take responsibility for such impulses, and do not ascribe them to our actual self, our will. Yet we ascribe to our will any tolerance of them, such as when our will allows them to influence our maxims to the detriment of its rational laws.

Practical reason, by thinking itself *into* a world of the mind, does not at all overstep its limits—as it would if it tried to enter that world *by way of intuition or sensation*. The world of the mind is only a negative idea *in relation to the world of sensation* in which there are no laws for our reason to determine the will. It is positive only on one point by combining a negative determination with a (positive) ability and even with a causality of reason. We may call this a will to act in such a way that the principle of the action conforms, in its essential nature, to a rational cause, namely the condition that the maxim of such actions be universally valid as a law. But if practical reason were to introduce, as an object of the will, a motive of action drawn from the intelligible world, then it would overstep its limits by presuming to be acquainted with what it cannot know.

The concept of an intelligible world, outside of appearances, is thus only a *viewpoint* from which reason sees itself *in order to think of itself as practical reason*. It could not do so if the influence of the sensory world were decisive for human beings. Yet it is necessary for us to see ourselves as intelligent beings, as a rational causality, active through reason and free in its operation. This thought brings about the idea of a law and order different from the idea that human beings are a mechanical contrivance of nature and of the world of senses. This requires the idea of an intelligible world (as a totality of rational beings as things in themselves). In this, there is not the slightest presumption to do anything more than point to a *formal* condition, to the universality of the will's maxims seen as laws and thus to the *autonomy* of the will. Only autonomy is thinkable as being consistent with freedom of the will. On the other hand, all laws determined by reference to some object must lead to heteronomy. This feature is found only in connection with the laws of nature and is applicable only to the world of sensation.

But reason would overstep all its limits if it undertook to *explain how* pure reason could be practical **[459]**, which is equivalent to the task of explaining how *freedom is possible*; for we can explain nothing other than what can be referred back to laws whose object can be rendered in some possible experience. Freedom is an idea whose objective reality can in no way be shown in terms of the laws of nature, and consequently not in any possible experience. It cannot be employed in any analogy that would produce an example because it cannot be conceptualized or be grasped by any insight. The idea of freedom can serve only as a necessary presupposition of reason in a being that believes itself conscious of having a will (capable of determining itself to act as an intelligent being according to the laws of reason, independently of natural instincts), and thus an ability that is different from the ability of desire.

Where determination according to natural laws ceases, there all *explanation* also ceases. Nothing remains but the *defense* of rejecting the objections of those who claim to have had deeper insight into the essence of things and who brazenly declare freedom to be impossible. We can only show them that the supposed contradiction they have discovered rests on nothing but this: in order to make the law of nature valid for human action, they have necessarily had to regard human beings as appearances—even after the demand has been made to think of them as intelligent beings and as things in themselves. Consequently, separating human causality (human will) from all natural laws of the sensory world must lead to a contradiction in regard to one and the same subject. But this contradiction would disappear if we would only realize that behind all appearances there must be grounds—things in themselves (however hidden they might be)—and that the laws governing the things themselves cannot be the same as the laws governing their appearances.

The subjective impossibility of *explaining* the freedom of the will is the same as the impossibility of discovering and explaining what *interest*[2] we can take in moral laws.
[460] Yet we do take an interest, based on what we might call our moral feeling. This has incorrectly been proclaimed as the standard for moral judgment. But it must be seen as the *subjective* effect that the law has on the will, while reason alone provides the *objective* grounds.

In order to will what reason alone prescribes as an *ought* to the sensually affected rational being, we need the ability to reason. This injects a feeling of pleasure or satisfaction at the fulfillment of duty. There is therefore a causality of reason to determine the sensory aspect according to its principles. Yet it is altogether impossible to see—to make it conceivable on an *a priori* basis—how a mere thought, which contains nothing sensuous, can bring forth a sensation of pleasure or displeasure; for this is a peculiar sort of causality from which we can determine nothing *a priori* (any more than in regard to any other causality) but must rely on experience.

Yet experience cannot provide us with a basis for the cause-and-effect relation, except between two objects of experience—although what we have here is nothing but pure reason functioning by means of mere ideas (which give us no objects of experience at all). Despite these objections, what we are after is the supposed cause of an effect in experience.

Apparently it is entirely out of the question for human beings to explain how and why the *universality of maxims as laws*, together with morality as a whole, should be of interest to us at all. This much is certain: that the moral law has validity for us not *because it is of interest* to us (for this amounts to heteronomy and dependence of practical reason on the senses, such as an underlying feeling, so that such reason could never be morally legislative) **[461]**; but it is of interest only because it is binding for us as human beings. It springs from our will as intelligent beings and therefore from our genuine self. But what belongs to mere appearance reason necessarily subordinates to the nature of the *thing itself.*

Therefore, the question of how a categorical imperative is possible can be answered, but only to the extent that we can point to the one presupposition under which the imperative is possible: the idea of freedom. The necessity of this presupposition is obvious—and it is sufficient for the *practical use* of reason for the conviction regarding *the validity of the imperative* and the moral law. Yet how this presupposition itself is possible cannot be grasped through any insight ever available to human reason. Despite all this, with the presupposition of the freedom of the will of an intelligent being, what necessarily follows is the *autonomy* of the will as the only formal precondition for determining that will.

As speculative philosophy can show, it is *possible* to presuppose this freedom of the will without falling into contradiction with the principle of nature's necessity in regard to the connection of appearances in the sensory world. Not only is this possible, it is also *necessary* to the practical aspect in a rational being who traces this causality to a consciousness of the will that makes freedom the underlying condition of all voluntary actions. How can pure reason, without other incentives that may be drawn from whatever source, be practical by itself? How can the bare

principle of the universal validity of all its maxims be taken
as law? This must certainly take the form of pure practical
reason. Without any further object to the will, which might
provide the basis of an interest that would be simply *moral*,
how could pure reason be practical? All of human reason is
quite insufficient to explain this, and all effort toward that
end would be in vain.

It is the same as if I tried to establish how freedom itself
is possible as the causality of a will. **[462]**   For with this I
leave the philosophic basis of explanation, and I have no
other. In the intelligible world that still remains to me, I
could indeed gad about among intelligent beings. But
although I may have an *idea* of such a world, an idea with its
own good grounds, I still do not have the least *acquaintance*
with such a world, nor can I ever achieve it, despite all the
efforts of my natural ability to reason. The idea of such an
intelligible world denotes merely something left over, after I
have excluded from the determinate grounds of my will
everything that belongs to the sensory world. The point of
this exercise is to restrict the principle of deriving all
motivation from the sensory field. By setting limits to this
field, I show that it does not contain everything in itself, but
that beyond the field of sense-experience there is more; with
this "more," however, I have no further acquaintance.

Of the realm of pure reason that thinks up this ideal
after the exclusion of all matter (the knowledge of objects),
nothing remains for me but the form. This is the practical
law of the universal validity of maxims. And along the lines
of this law I think of reason in its relation to an intelligible
world, as a possible effective cause, as a cause that
determines the will. No incentive can work here, unless this
idea of an intelligible world would itself be the incentive, or
that in which reason originally took an interest. Although it
is our task to make this conceivable, this is precisely the
problem we cannot solve.

Here, then, is the extreme boundary to all moral inquiry.
Defining that boundary is of great importance—first, so that
our reason may not waste its effort in searching through the
world of sensation, to the detriment of morals, looking for a
supreme motive and a comprehensible but empirical interest;
and second, so that our reason may not stray feebly into the
empty space of transcendental concepts that we call the
intelligible world without advancing from its initial position
but rather losing itself in figments of the imagination.

The idea of a pure world of the mind as the unity of
intelligent beings remains as a useful and legitimate idea in
the service of rational belief. We belong to it as rational
beings (although at the same time we belong to the world of

the senses). By describing the noble ideal of a universal realm of *ends in themselves* (for rational beings) we can be members of this realm when we scrupulously **[463]** conduct ourselves according to maxims of freedom—as though these were laws of nature. And although all knowledge reaches its limit here, this universal realm serves to stimulate in us a lively interest in moral law.

Concluding Note

The *speculative* use of reason *in regard to nature* leads us to the absolute necessity of a supreme cause *of the world*. The *practical* use of reason *with its purpose of freedom* also leads to an absolute necessity, but only to the necessity of the *laws of action* of a rational being as such.

Now it is an essential principle, for every use of our reason, to push its knowledge to the point at which we are conscious of its *necessity* (for without such necessity it would not be knowledge originating from reason). But it is also an equally essential *restriction* of the same reason that it can have no insight into the *necessity* of what is, or what happens, or what ought to happen, except on the basis of a precondition under which it is or happens or ought to happen. However, we repeatedly put off satisfaction of our reason by the constant inquiry regarding such precondition.

Accordingly, reason tirelessly searches for the unconditioned and the necessary. Moreover, it sees itself compelled to assume it, though without any means for making it comprehensible. Reason is happy enough when it can find a concept that is compatible with this presupposition. And if reason cannot make comprehensible the absolute necessity of an unconditioned practical law (such as the categorical imperative must be), this is not the fault of our deduction of the supreme principle of morality, but it is rather a reproach that can be leveled against human reason in general. It is not a drawback of reason that it resists offering an explanation by means of a condition, relying on some sort of interest—for in that case the law would no longer be a moral law, a supreme law of freedom.

Thus we do not comprehend the practical unconditioned necessity of the moral imperative; but we do comprehend its *incomprehensibility*—and this is all we can fairly demand of a philosophy which, in its principles, strives to reach the limit of human reason.

NOTES

[1] For our purposes only, I am suggesting this approach of accepting freedom as the basis of the actions of rational beings only *in idea*, so that I don't find myself obligated to prove it also in its theoretical intent; for even if we have the latter unresolved, the same laws apply to a being that cannot act other than under the idea of its own freedom as would apply to a being that is truly free. So we would be relieved of the burden that, in this case, imposes itself on the theory.

[2] Reason becomes practical through interest, i.e. a cause   which determines the will. We say about a rational being that it takes an interest in something, while a non-rational being can feel only a sensory impulse. Reason takes a direct interest in an action only if the universality of the action's maxim is a sufficiently determinant ground of the will. Only such an action is pure. But if reason determines the will through another object of desire or some special feeling on the part of the subject, then reason has only an indirect interest in the action. Reason, on its own and without relying on experience, has no way of discovering objects of will or underlying feelings; thus the interest, here, would be empirical and not purely rational. Reason's logical interest (to enlarge its sphere of insight) is never direct, but assumes implicit aims reason might serve.